#53

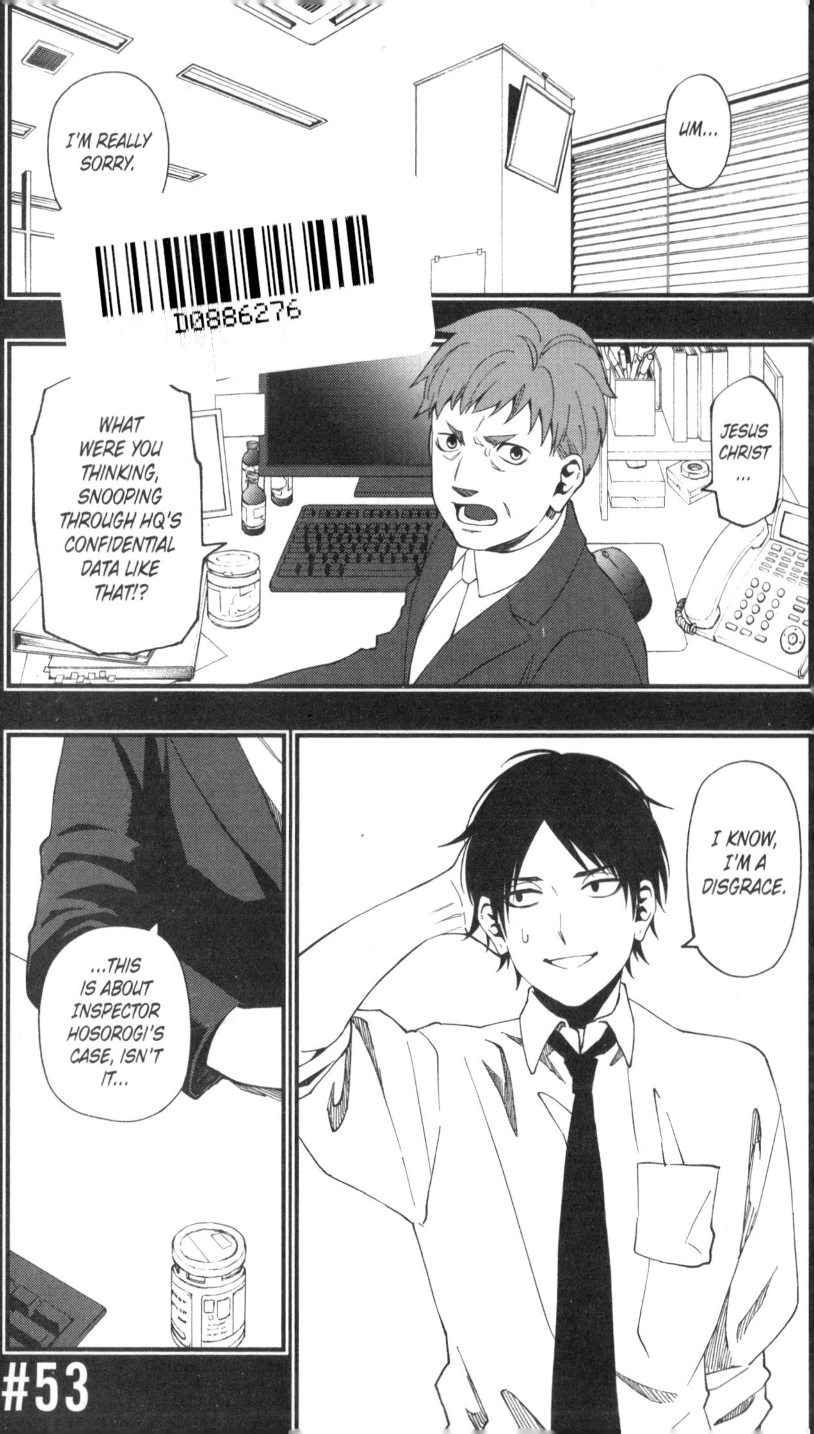
UM...
I'M REALLY SORRY.
JESUS CHRIST ...
WHAT WERE YOU THINKING, SNOOPING THROUGH HQ'S CONFIDENTIAL DATA LIKE THAT!?
I KNOW, I'M A DISGRACE.
...THIS IS ABOUT INSPECTOR HOSOROGI'S CASE, ISN'T IT...

...!

THAT'S... BUT—

QUIT GETTING SO INVOLVED OVER SOMEONE WHO'S NOT EVEN AROUND ANYMORE.

YOU'VE GOT TO MOVE ON FOR THOSE WHO ARE GONE TOO.

I'M TELLING YOU TO KEEP YOUR EYES ON THE FUTURE.

......

WAS IT...... YOUR DAUGHTER?

I'M JUST TELLING YOU AS...... SOMEONE WITH EXPERI- ENCE.

...I'M NOT TRYING TO BE MEAN.

THAT'S HOW I MADE IT THIS FAR.

YES...... I DECIDED I'D MAKE THE MOST OF LIFE FOR THE BOTH OF US.

......
......I'M SORRY.

...FOR MY DAUGHTER'S SAKE, NOT JUST MY OWN.

LISTEN... IWANOME.

I'M LIVING MY LIFE...

AND I INTEND TO FULFILL MY DUTIES UNTIL MY DYING BREATH.

#53

HABAKI-SAN.

...YOU'RE REALLY SOMETHING.

CONTENTS

DEAD MOUNT
DEATH PLAY

7

DEAD MOUNT DEATH PLAY

STORY RYOHGO NARITA
ART SHINTA FUJIMOTO

... DAUGHTER?

MEKI
(KRIK)

メキ

DID YOU EVEN MEAN ANY OF IT!?

WHAT HAPPENED TO LIVING FOR YOUR DAUGHTER...?

ZUZU
(LOOM)
ズ ズ

UH...

WHOA, NOW...

...I'D JUST GIVE IT UP!?

YOU THINK THAT AFTER I WENT SO FAR AS TO SACRIFICE MY DAUGHTER TO GET HERE...

A...

...LIE?

BAKYA
(KRAAK)

YOU GOTTA BE KIDDING ME!

HNGH ...!

GA
(KICK)

CALM DOWN, SIR.

GUGU
(PUSH)

YEAH. YOU'VE GOT A POINT THERE.

...

THIS IS STILL BETTER THAN LEMMINGS, RIGHT?

YOU GOT IT.

I'LL THANK YOU LATER.

FOR NOW, I'M GONNA NEED YOUR HELP, ARASE.

DO (WHAM)

BATA (THMP) BATA

HM?

I STARTED TO GET SUSPICIOUS WHEN I PASSED AN OFFICER ACTING ODD...

YOU OKAY, IWA-SAN!?

YATSU ...!

NICE MOVE, BUT I'LL THANK YOU LATER!

I SCRAPED TOGETHER EVERYONE I COULD FROM COMPS-3. WE'RE NOT INTERRUPTING ANYTHING, ARE WE?

SENIOR COMMIS- SIONER HABAKI!?

WHOA, WHOA.

WHA...?

GASHA (CRASH)

WHAT THE...!?

YOU DON'T SAY...

SO, MANAGER, WHAT'S HE BEING CHARGED WITH?

GLAD YOU'RE SO QUICK ON THE UPTAKE.

IT'S ABOUT HOSO- ROGI- SAN.

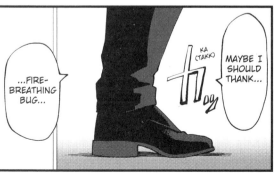

...FIRE- BREATHING BUG...

KA (TAKK)

MAYBE I SHOULD THANK...

A PHONE CALL? TO WHOM!?

THAT "HIGURO" GUY? OR SOMEONE ELSE...?

!

THANKS TO YOU... I MADE IT IN TIME.

ON IT!

ズ∞
SU (SSK)

ARASE!

ぶ ん
BUN (TOSS)

ぱし
PASHI (SNATCH)

!?

フ
FU (FFFD)

ッ

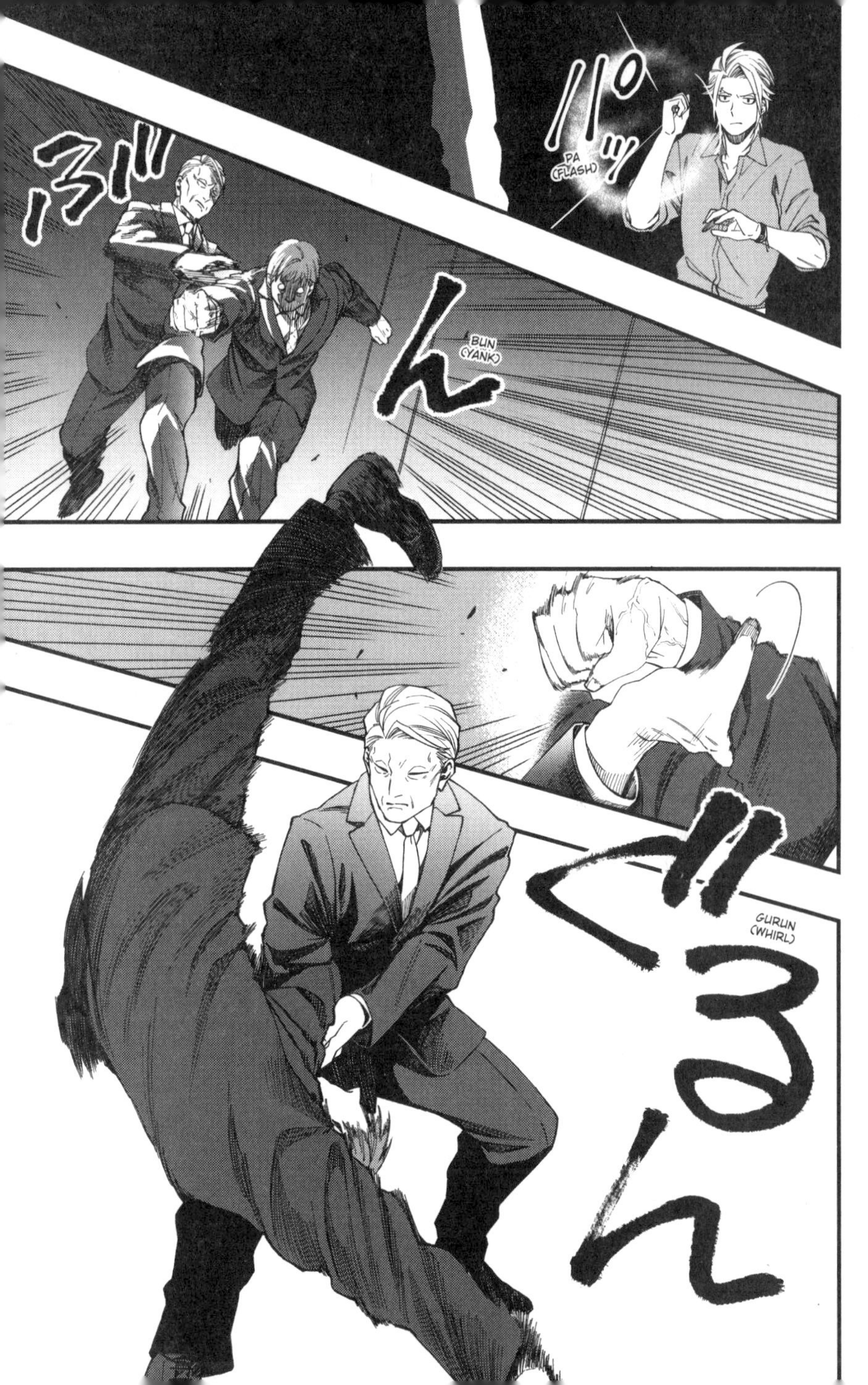
パッ
PA (FLASH)
ぶ
ん
BUN (YANK)
ぐるん
GURUN (WHIRL)

WE'RE IN THE PRE-CINCT...

...WITH PERMISSION TO CARRY.

A GUN!?

HE'S AIMING FOR—

THAT'S IT! KEEP THAT UP—

!

GET OUT OF THERE, POPS!

......!

PAN
(BLAM)

DA
(DASH)

DOSA
(THUD)

I OWE YOU ONE!

OOF!

SOMETHING TELLS ME... THAT WASN'T A MISFIRE.

...ON THE OTHER SIDE OF THE BEYOND.

WE'LL MEET AGAIN...

YES, SIR!

...... GOOD WORK.

HE WAS AT *THAT* BUILDING DURING THE SHINJUKU MUGGING INVESTIGATION......

!?

I KNOW THAT GUY!

GASHA (SMASH)

HEY! WHAT ARE YOU DOING—

DAMN IT! HE DIDN'T—

DON'T ...!

!?

PAN
(BANG)

...YATSU, YOU AND POPS GO AFTER SENIOR COMMISSIONER HABAKI!

WHA...? WHAT THE HELL IS GOING ON, IWA-SAN!?

CHIKA
(CLICK)

4.11

DA
(DASH)

PA
(FLASH)

!

I GUESS THIS IS THE END OF THE ROAD.

THESE GUYS ARE STILL...!

OH!

...BURN THE RIGHTEOUS.

I DON'T WISH TO...

...THIS FEELS FAMILIAR.

...

THIS IS...

HEY! WHY AM I BEING ARRESTED...!?

WAIT, WHERE AM I...?

OWW...!

"...ONCE THE FLAMES BROKE OUT, WHY DIDN'T YOU GUYS MOVE A MUSCLE FOR A FEW SECONDS?"

"WE WEREN'T ABLE TO MAKE OUT MUCH ON THE CAR RECORDER DUE TO SOME STRANGE AUDIO INTERFERENCE, BUT..."

JUST LIKE WHEN THAT FAKE FIRE-BREATHING BUG WAS KILLED IN THAT BLAST...

"IT WAS LIKE TEN SECONDS JUST SUDDENLY FLEW BY..."

"...AND THE NEXT THING I KNOW, HE'S ON FIRE."

"I JUST, WELL...ONE MINUTE I'M GETTING THIS UNRULY SUSPECT UNDER CONTROL..."

"WELL... SEE, I DON'T KNOW EITHER..."

ASSUMING THESE GUYS AREN'T FAKING IT...

YOU FIGURED SOMETHING OUT, DIDN'T YOU?

COULD IT BE...... THIS WAS THE REASON?

SOMETHING JUST OUTSIDE THE REALM OF COMMON SENSE...

...THE FIRE-BREATHING BUG MUST BE ONE PERSON, AND YET NOT ONE PERSON.

A HYPNOTIST... PERHAPS?

UMBRELLA: WATCH OUT FOR FIRES

ROGER THAT!

WE SHOULD SPLIT UP AND SEARCH.

...IF WE CAN'T ARRANGE FOR BACK-UP, IT'LL BE HARD TO SECURE HIM...

...

AW, DAMN IT.

WHAT'S KOCHOU GONNA TELL ME LATER...

DA (DASH)

TH-THIS... HAS TO BE THE PLACE...

HFF!

HFF!

22

BA
(TURN)

YO, HABAKI.

OHH... OHH...!

I CAN'T BELIEVE IT'S REALLY YOU!

WHEN DID YOU GET TO JAPAN!?

ANYWAY, WHILE I WAS LOOKING FOR A HOTEL...

I JUST GOT IN TODAY.

...I HEARD THAT HQ GOT AN EMERGENCY CALL FROM YOU.

...THERE'S NO NEED TO THANK ME.

YOU'VE DONE GOOD WORK SO FAR.

I EXPECT YOU TO KEEP IT UP.

AHH... YOU'RE TOO GOOD TO ME.

THAT POWER OUTAGE— YOU DID THAT FOR OUR SAKE!?

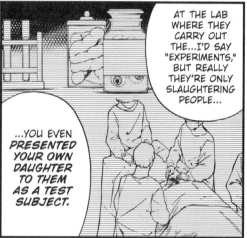

AT THE LAB WHERE THEY CARRY OUT THE...I'D SAY "EXPERIMENTS," BUT REALLY THEY'RE ONLY SLAUGHTERING PEOPLE...

...YOU EVEN *PRESENTED YOUR OWN DAUGHTER TO THEM AS A TEST SUBJECT.*

...YES, SPEAKING OF GOOD WORK.

YOU'VE MANAGED TO BRING ALL SORTS OF GOODIES TO THE ORGANI-ZATION.

HMM ......

THANK YOU FOR THE KIND WORDS!

I'M SURE MY DAUGHTER IS REJOICING FROM BEYOND THE GRAVE...!

WHEN I SAID "YOU'VE DONE GOOD WORK SO FAR"...

...I WASN'T TALKING ABOUT YOU.

...AND "I EXPECT YOU TO KEEP IT UP"...

HUH?

HABAKI...... YOU'RE MISTAKEN ON TWO COUNTS.

WHAT...?

AND YOUR SECOND MISTAKE—

DIDN'T I TELL YOU? "THERE'S NO NEED TO THANK ME."

I WAS JUST ABOUT READY TO ABANDON YOU COMPLETELY.

HUH? I DON'T FOLLOW...

25

!?

...IS AN EXPRESSION USED ONLY FOR THE DEAD, ISN'T IT?

"FROM BEYOND THE GRAVE"...

DO (CRUNCH)

DOSHA (SMASH)

... SHITTY DAD.

IT'S BEEN A WHILE...

... SOARA ...

... AREN'T YOU?

YOU'RE ...

N...

N-NO...

IT CAN'T BE.

LITTLE SOARA HABAKI-CHAN.

THAT'S RIGHT.

YOU NEVER EVEN TRIED TO GET TO KNOW HER, SO WE NEVER TOLD YOU.

BUT CONGRATULATIONS ON YOUR DAUGHTER BEING THE FIRST CASE TO SURVIVE THE EXPERIMENTS.

OR MORE ACCU-RATELY ...

...THE ILLEGITIMATE CHILD YOU COULDN'T BE BOTHERED TO RAISE, SO YOU TOSSED HER.

THE DAUGHTER YOU GAVE OVER TO OUR ORGANIZATION, BASTARD CHILDREN OF SABARAMOND.

AND SHE'S ASKED ME FOR A SPECIAL FAVOR.

SHE PERSONALLY WANTS TO EXECUTE...

...THE FATHER WHO TREATED HER LIKE A GUINEA PIG.

SHE RANKS HIGHER EVEN THAN YOU NOW.

CODENAME— ARAHABAKI.

Y...

YOU MON-STEEER!

I'LL CUT INTO YOU JUST AS MUCH AS THEY CUT INTO ME.

I'VE THOUGHT ABOUT YOU ALL THIS TIME, DEAR FATHER.

W-WAIT...

GUSHA (CRUNCH)

AWW, WHAT A TOUCHING FATHER-DAUGHTER REUNION.

ZAAAAA (FSHHH)

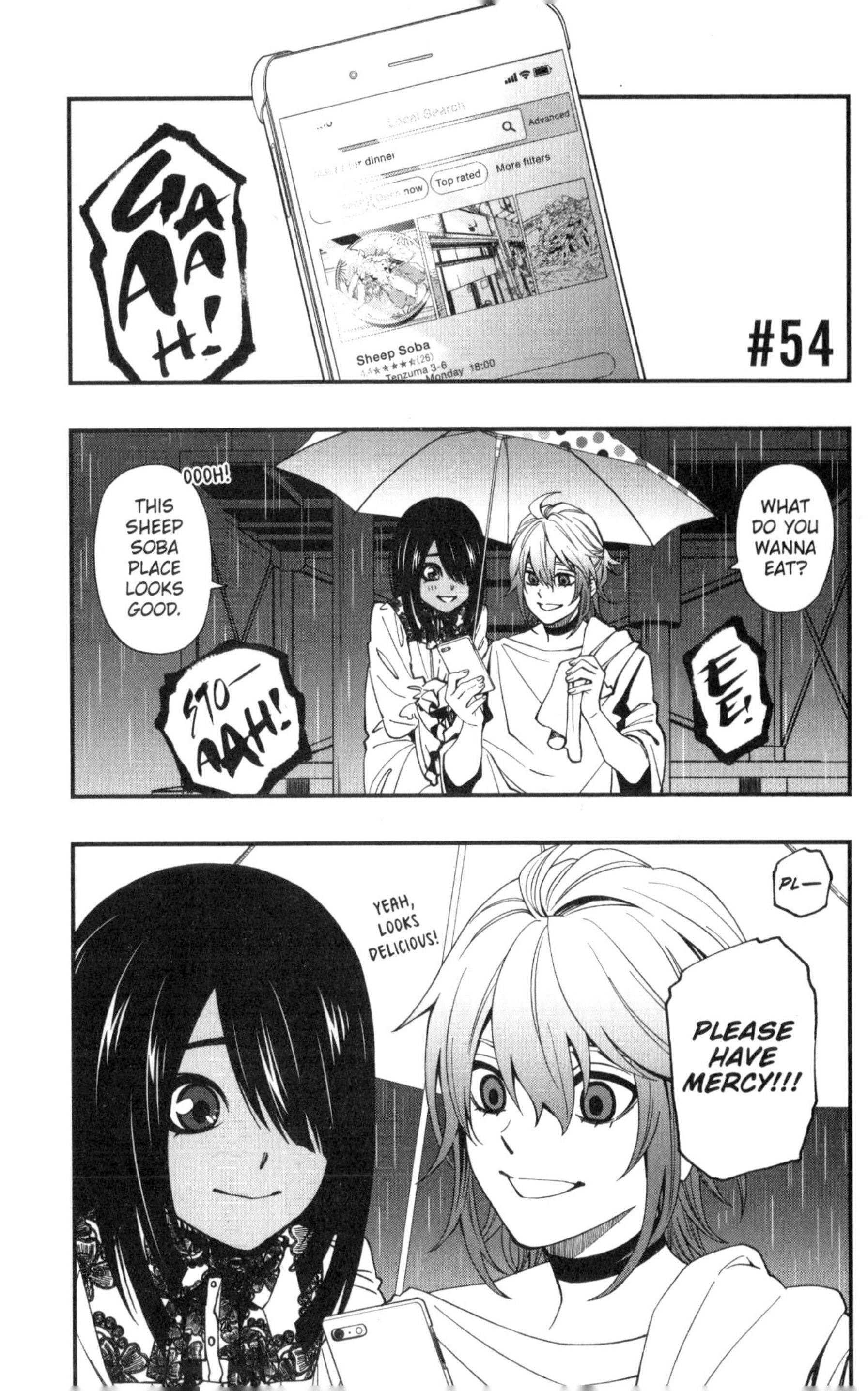
#54
Local Search
Advanced
dinner
Open now
Top rated
More filters
Sheep Soba
(26)
Tenzuma 3-6
Monday 18:00
GAAAH!
WHAT DO YOU WANNA EAT?
EE!
OOOH!
THIS SHEEP SOBA PLACE LOOKS GOOD.
STO— AAH!
PL—
PLEASE HAVE MERCY!!!
YEAH, LOOKS DELICIOUS!

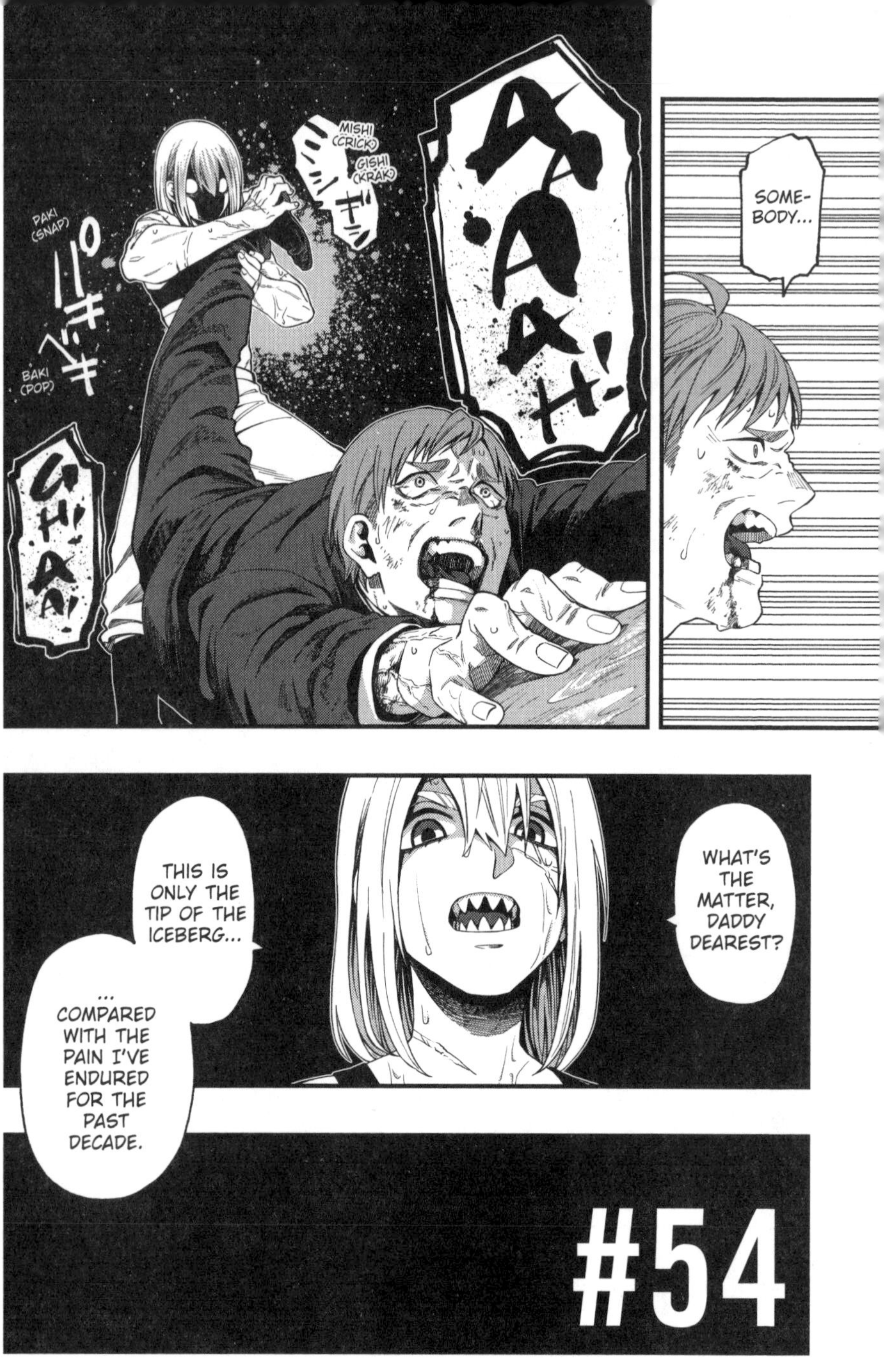
SOME-BODY...
AAAH!
MISHI (CRICK)
GISHI (KRAK)
PAKI (SNAP)
BAKI (POP)
UGHAA!
WHAT'S THE MATTER, DADDY DEAREST?
THIS IS ONLY THE TIP OF THE ICEBERG...
... COMPARED WITH THE PAIN I'VE ENDURED FOR THE PAST DECADE.
#54

ONLY AFTER YOU TOLD ME THAT HORRIBLE LAB...

...WAS A PLACE "LIKE A PARADISE."

OH, IS THAT HOW YOU REMEMBER IT?

B-BUT YOU SAID YOU'D GIVE UP YOUR BODY FOR ME...

EVEN JUST ONCE WOULD'VE BEEN FINE.

ONCE.

GO

A!

BAKI

GA (WHAK)

E!

GA 00!

GO

GO, (BASH)

I'VE MADE UP MY MIND.

GWA!

...HAD COME TO CHECK ON ME AFTER THE FACT...

IF YOU...

LUCKY FOR ME...

...YOU'RE A COLD-HEARTED BASTARD.

GUGH...

...THEN I'D SPARE YOUR LIFE.

THAT'S OUR TARGET FOR TODAY.

THAT'S HIM.

34

I CAN STILL BE OF USE TO THE ORGANIZATION... TO THE BASTARD CHILDREN OF SABARAMOND!

JUST GIVE ME SOME TIME AND... I'LL FIND YOU THE SORCERER WHO CAME FROM THE OTHER SIDE OF THE SKY...!

I-I CAN STILL MAKE IT UP TO YOU!

THERE'S NO WAY YOU COULD DO THAT.

NAH.

HMM...

TH-THAT'S NOT TRUE...!! PLEASE JUST GIVE ME A CHANCE!

WHAT!? THAT WASN'T WHAT WE AGREED, BOSS!

NGH! R-REALLY...!?

I DON'T MIND GIVING YOU ANOTHER SHOT...

I DON'T THINK YOU FULLY GRASP THE SITUATION YOU'RE IN.

THING IS, YOU'LL NEVER CHANGE.

GIRI (GRIP)

NOW, NOW. HEAR ME OUT.

I THINK YOU'VE MADE IT PRETTY FAR BY ONLY LOOKING AHEAD.

HA-BAKI.

N-NO! I SWEAR I WILL...

...OR THIS VERY MOMENT.

LIKE, FOR INSTANCE, WHEN IT COMES TO SOARA...

BUT REALLY, YOU SHOULD'VE SPARED AT LEAST A GLANCE BEHIND YOU.

HUH?

WHAT DO—

BLRGH!

PASHIN (BANG)

(GYUO)
(WHIRL)

...HUH?

CLEAN HEAD-SHOT.

WE CAN IGNORE THE GIRL WITH HIM.

WAS THAT A HIT?

SO WHY HIRE US JUST TO SNIPE THAT BATTERED OLD GEEZER...?

I MEAN, AREN'T WE THE TOP KILLERS IN SHIBUYA?

STILL... I CAN'T BELIEVE SHE WANTED TO TEST THE SKILLS OF THE HOROJIMA SIBLINGS.

MAKES YOU WONDER...

...WHAT'S THE STORY BEHIND THE SHINJUKU MEDIATORS' "PETTY REVENGE."

コト
KOTO (CLINK)

YES, MA'AM!

I'M HEADED OUT. COULD YOU GET THINGS READY?

ZAAAA CFSHHHHH

DUO

...ARA-HABAKI.

YOU'VE GOT THREE MINUTES...

SURE THING.

...BOSS.

GIVE ME MY ORDERS.

ZAAAAA

40

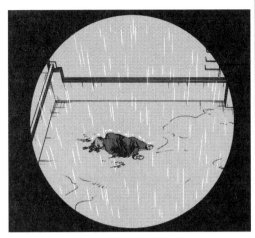

Sicut vis.
<AS YOU WISH.>

GREAT...

HUH?

MM.

TOO LATE.

...LET'S PULL OUT OF HERE, QUICK.

OR AT LEAST LAY LOW ON THE MIDDLE FLOOR...

WHAT IS IT?

SHE'S COMING RIGHT FOR US.

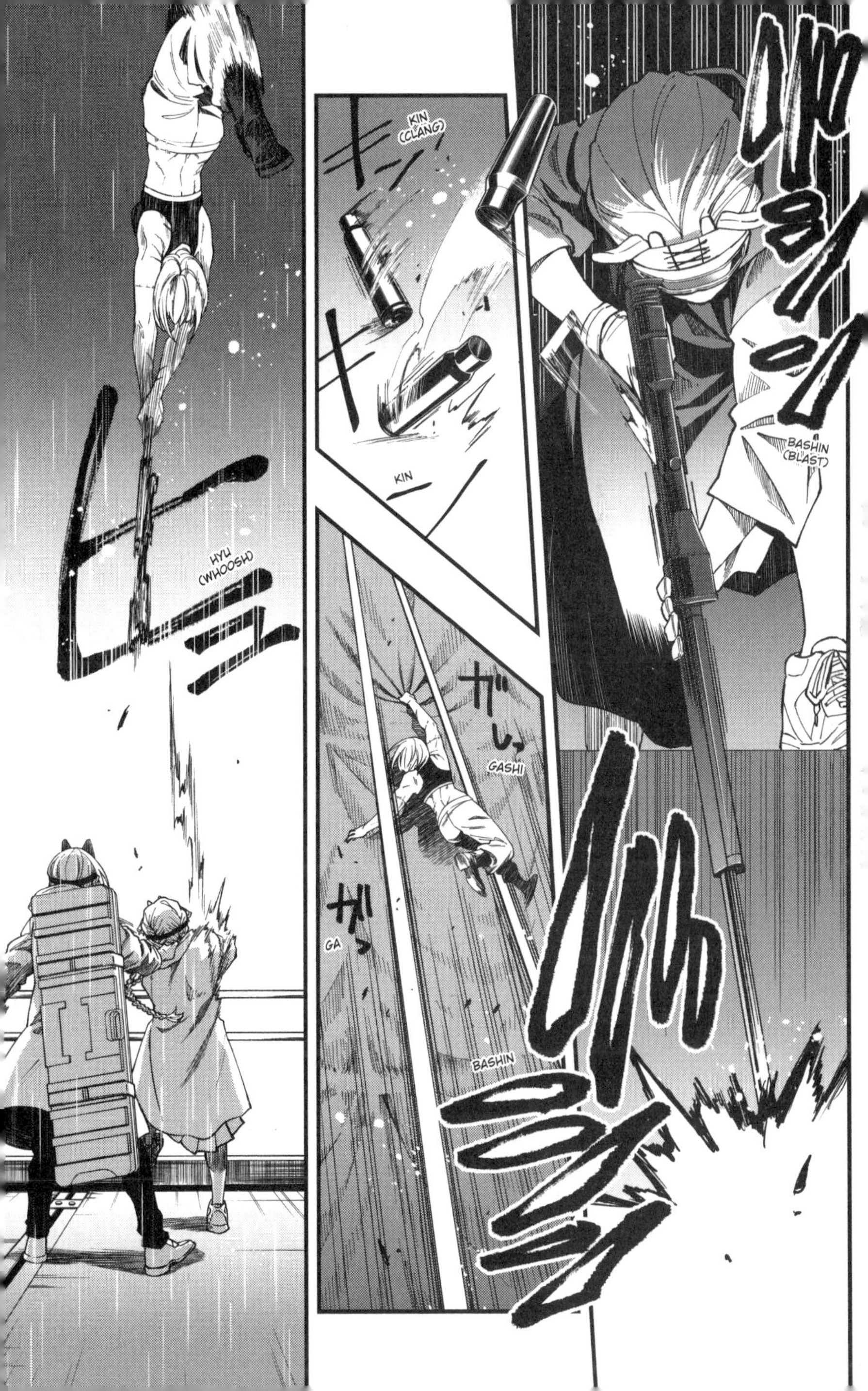
BASHIN (BLAST)
KIN (CLANG)
KIN
GASHI
GA
BASHIN
HYU (WHOOSH)

YOU'VE REALLY GONE AND DONE IT NOW...

...LITTLE PEEPING TOMS.

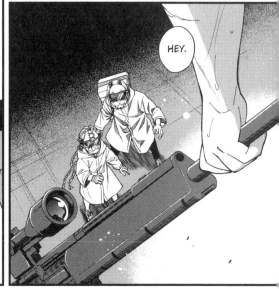

HEY.

TAN (LEAP)

GA (CLANG)

......!

DA (DASH)

DOSU (THUD)

MEKI (KRIK)
PAKI (KRAK)

LOOKS LIKE WE'RE GONNA DIE HERE.

AW, MAN...

NOW WE'RE UP SHIT CREEK.

I COULD CRY.

PASHA (SPLISH)

PASHA

I WAS ONLY ABLE TO HURT HIM......HALF AS MUCH AS I WANTED TO, YOU SEE......?

GASHA (CLATTER)

...HALF.

?

...SO YOU'RE GONNA MAKE IT UP TO ME, GOT IT?

YOU TOOK MY LIFE'S REVENGE FROM ME...

...MOCKING US?

ARE YOU...

HMM.

OR...I CAN ALWAYS TAKE IT UP WITH YOUR CLIENT IF YOU TELL ME WHO HIRED YOU. DEAL?

CHA CCHK?

...IF THOSE MEASLY GUNS...

...ARE ENOUGH TO TAKE DOWN AN ANIMAL LIKE ME.

NO, I'M NOT. A PAIR AS SKILLED AS YOU MUST KNOW...

46

HAH!

DON (BLAM)

GOOD ONE.

PASHA (SPLASH)

WERE YOU AIMING FOR MY EYE?

TO (GTHD)

YOU'LL BE WELL WORTH DESTROY- ING.

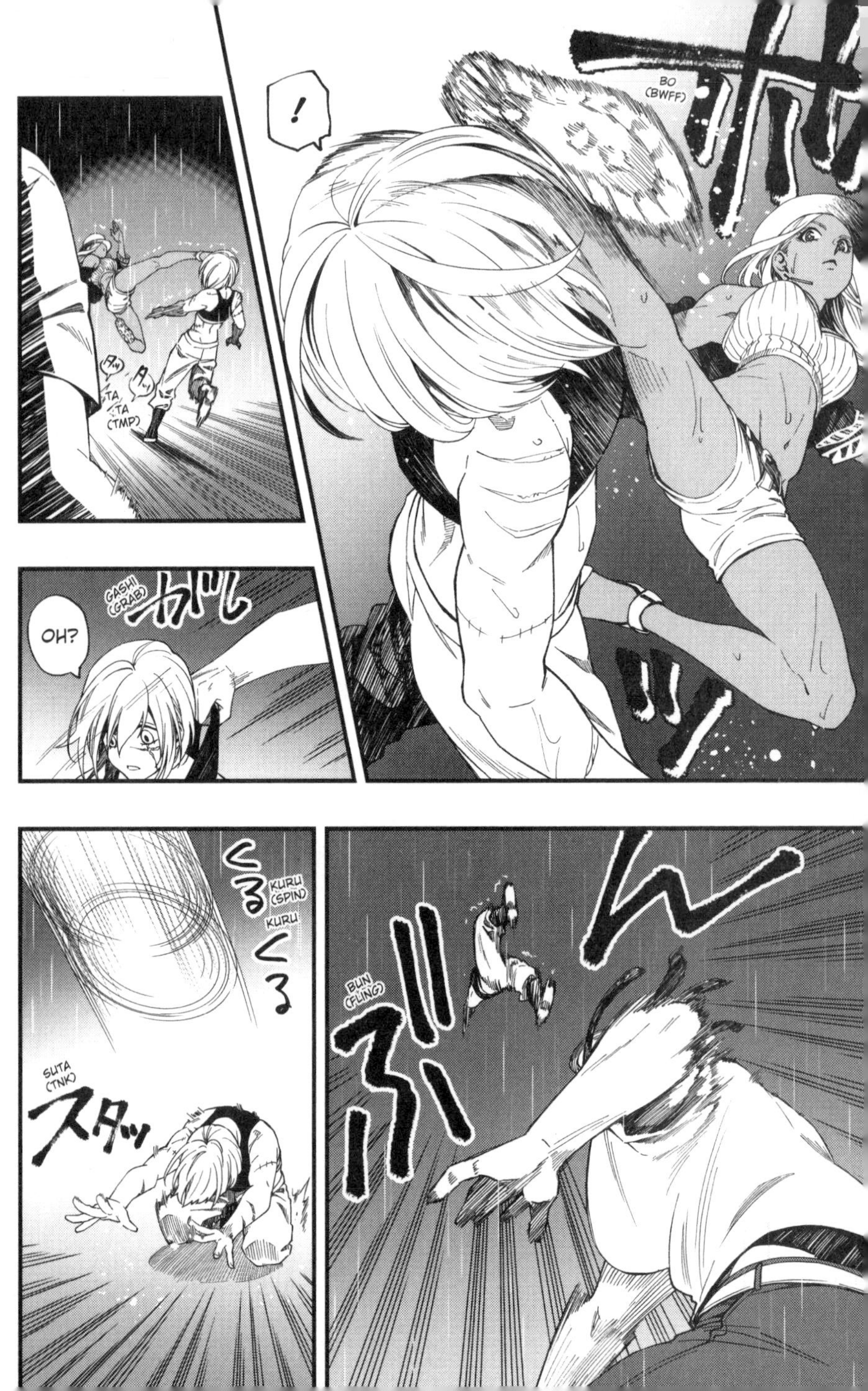
BO (BWFF)
!
TA
TA (TMP)
GASHI (GRAB)
OH?
BUN (FLING)
KURU (SPIN)
KURU
SUTA (TNK)

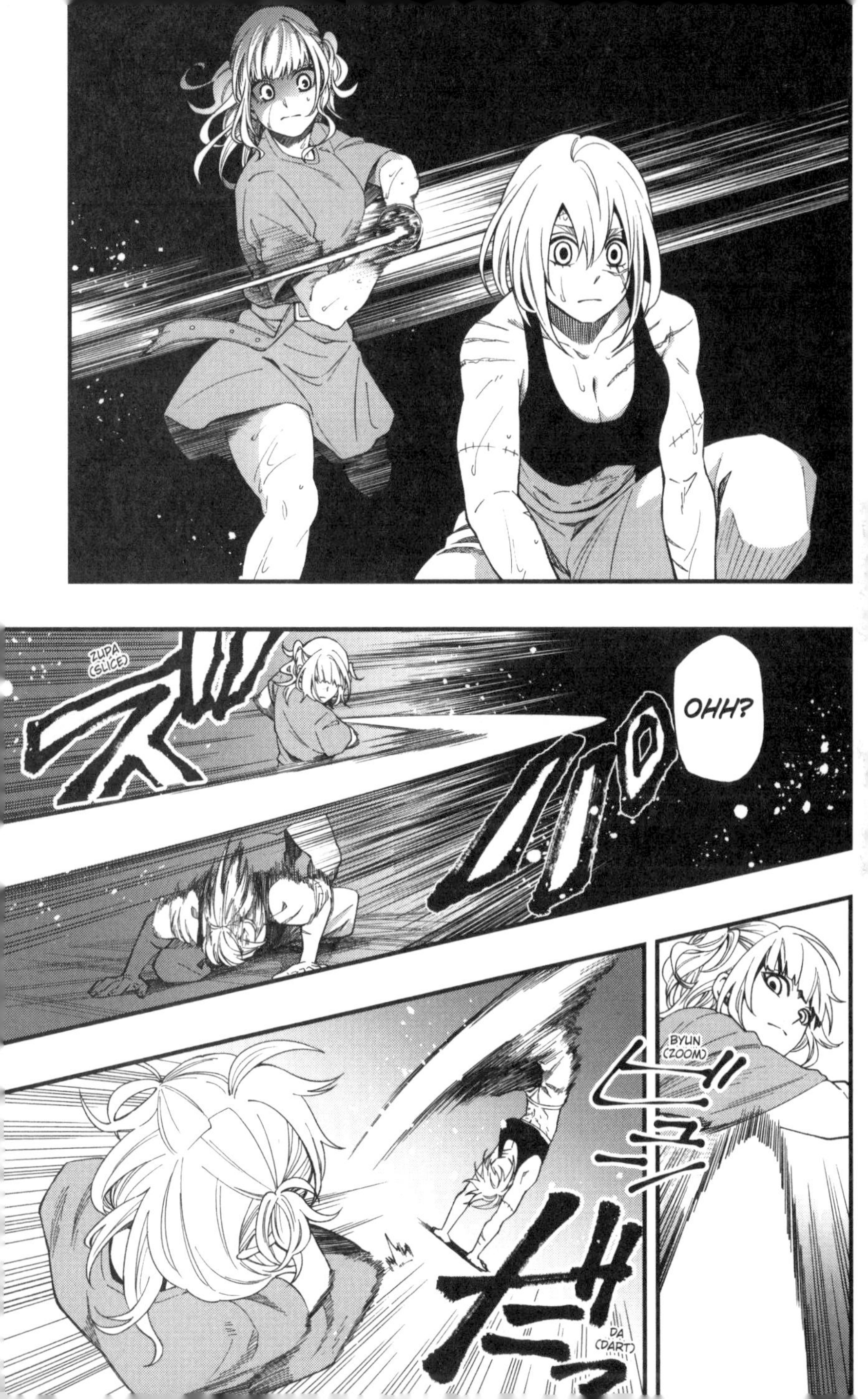
ZUPA
(SLICE)
OHH?
BYUN
(ZOOM)
DA
(DART)

SO THERE'S A WHOLE FAMILY OF YOU PEEPING TOMS...

...HM?

TCH.

WAIT...... DOES THIS MEAN YOU'VE BEEN KEEPING WATCH OVER US?

IS THIS FOR ALL THE BACKSTABBING AND RUNNING AWAY AND STUFF?

......CLARISSA ISN'T SO FOOLISH SHE'D LEAVE ROOKIES ON THEIR OWN.

THEY'RE FROM...

BUT THANK YOU...

...FOR SAVING US.

WHY, YOU...

PUI (POUT)

I REALLY DON'T LIKE HER.

HNN.

DANG, SHE'S PRETTY CUTE.

SO CUTE.

SO CUTE.

SO CUTE.

I'VE GOT A CUTIE IN MY GANG TOO!

CHIRA (GLANCE)

???

ACK......! DON'T THINK I'LL FORGIVE YOU JUST 'COS YOU'RE CUTE!

ACK!?

HAS IT ALREADY BEEN *THREE MINUTES*!?

WHERE'D THEY GO!?

HUH?

?

?

?

RRRRGH! YOU GOTTA BE KIDDING ME!

YOU THINK WE'LL LET YOU JUST WALK AWAY?

...SHOOT. LOOKS LIKE I'LL HAVE TO RETURN TO THE GUARD.

52

LETTING ME GET AWAY, THAT IS!

GURA
(SWAY)

I THINK THAT'D BE BETTER FOR YOU, DON'T YOU?

......!

GARA
(CLATTER)

GARA

HYOI
(LIFT)

GASHA
(CRASH)

NO WAY! FOR REAL!?

SHE'S GOTTA BE LEMMINGS'S LEVEL!

GA
(CLANG)

IS SHE SAYING THERE ARE OTHERS WHO CAN DO WHAT I DO?

LEM-MINGS...?

AAAH!

N CGRIND

GUESS I'M GONNA HAVE SOME FUN AFTER ALL...

...IN THIS CITY.

KON

KON
(KNOCK)

THE COLOR OF THEIR SPIRIT IS......

......MISAKI AND THE OTHERS DON'T KNOCK.

WHO COULD IT BE?

I APOLOGIZE FOR DROPPING BY SO LATE.

GACHA
(KCHAK)

CLARISSA-SAN...

THERE'S...... SOMEBODY I DESPERATELY WANT TO ASK A QUESTION OF.

I NEED YOUR POWERS.

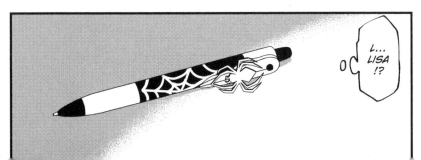

L... LISA !?

... YES.

THIS IS MY FIRST TIME MEETING YOU.

YOU ARE SAYO SHINO-YAMA-CHAN... I TAKE IT?

YOU KNOW ABOUT ME?

JUST THAT YOU'RE POLKA-KUN'S FAMILY.

SAYO-SAN AND ROZA-SAN KNOW ABOUT CORPSE GOD... JUST THEM, THOUGH.

AH... CLARISSA-SAN.

...JUST BE CAREFUL, OKAY?

WELL, YOU'RE FREE TO TELL THEM AS MUCH AS YOU LIKE, BUT...

...I SEE.

YOU'RE THE SON OF THE WEALTHY SHINOYAMA EMPIRE...

IF WHOEVER WAS TARGETING *POLKA SHINOYAMA* FOUND OUT, IT'D LEAD TO ALL SORTS OF TROUBLE.

DON'T FORGET— YOU HAVE THAT SCAR ON YOUR NECK BECAUSE *SOMEONE TRIED TO TAKE YOUR LIFE* ONCE BEFORE ALREADY.

#55

WHAT IS IT?

Shinoyam

F Presi

F Offic

...HAVE BEEN CONTACTED BY THE MEDIATORS.

POLKA SHINOYAMA AND YOUR LITTLE SISTER...

...I SEEK INSTRUC-TIONS.

SHE ONLY BROUGHT ALONG ONE ASSOCIATE.

A NOVICE, BY THE LOOK OF HER.

GREAT. JUST WHAT I NEED.

......LISA KURAKI.

IF THEY MAKE ANY MOVES, SPLIT UP YOUR FORCES AND FOLLOW THEM.

...I SEE. WELL, JUST BE ON THE ALERT.

IF YOU GET A WHIFF OF ANY FOUL PLAY, DON'T WAIT FOR MY SIGNAL. MAKE YOUR MOVE.

Are you sure?

IF THIS IS LISA KURAKI WE'RE DEALING WITH, SHE'S ALREADY AWARE OF YOUR PRESENCE.

...As you wish.

LISA
KURAKI
......

WHAT ON
EARTH IS
SHE UP
TO?

ZAAAA
(FSHHH)

POLKA-
KUN......
OR
RATHER,
CORPSE
GOD.

GOOD.
THEN IT
SHOULD
BE OKAY IF
WE SPEAK
HERE.

...I'LL
BE
CARE-
FUL.

WOULD
YOU PLEASE
COME WITH
ME?

I HAVE
A "JOB"
TO ASK
OF
YOU.

OH, I DON'T THINK YOU'LL HAVE TO WORRY ABOUT HER.

...I THINK SOMETHING'S HAPPENED TO TAKUMI-KUN AND THE OTHERS.

SO I DON'T WANT TO LEAVE SAYO-SAN ALONE...

CHIRA (GLANCE)

ちらちら

SURE, BUT...

POTSUN (ALONE)

ぽ   つん

NOW LET'S GO.

O-OKAY.

?

......THE ELDEST DAUGHTER OF THE SHINOYAMA FAMILY HAS BEEN LEFT ON HER OWN.

PLEASE PROTECT HER WITH YOUR LIFE UNTIL MY ASSOCIATE GETS BACK.

PASHA (SPLASH)

パシャ

ZAAAA (FSHHH)

アアー

東京都公安委
Tokyo Metropolitan P

警視庁本部庁舎
Metropolitan Police Department Headquarters

警視庁
Metropolitan Police

HMPH...

...WILY FOX.

NOT TO MENTION, A GUN WAS FIRED AT AN INSPECTOR...

...BEFORE THE SUSPECT TURNED IT ON HIM-SELF.

OFFICERS WHO WERE NOT IN THEIR RIGHT MINDS WENT ON A RAMPAGE.

SOLITAIRE WAS ALLOWED TO BREAK INTO MY OFFICE.

EP-OUT 警視庁 立入禁止 KEEP OUT 警視庁 立入禁止

OUR TERRITORY HAS BEEN INTRUDED ON FAR TOO MUCH IN TOO MANY WAYS FOR ONE SINGLE DAY.

KA CTHWAK

SOMEONE TAMPERED WITH THE ELECTRICAL SYSTEM...

...AND DURING THE BLACKOUT, BOTH SOLITAIRE AND HABAKI GOT AWAY... IS WHAT YOU'RE SAYING.

...I HADN'T NARROWED IT DOWN TO HIM FOR SURE.

BUT I'VE KNOWN FOR A WHILE NOW THAT THERE WAS A TRAITOR AMONG UPPER MANAGEMENT.

...SUPER-INTENDENT GENERAL, DID YOU SUSPECT SENIOR COMMISSIONER HABAKI FROM THE START?

UMM...

......!! DO YOU MEAN TO SAY...?

EVEN THOUGH FIVE YEARS AGO...... I WAS ONE STEP AWAY FROM FINALLY TRACKING THEM DOWN.

I WAS PROBABLY BEING MONITORED BY THEM TOO.

THAT WAS INSPECTOR MIYABI HOSOROGI.

......THE ONE WHO WAS CLOSEST TO CRACKING IT DISAPPEARED ALONG WITH THE EVIDENCE.

......

ZAAAA (FSHHH)

...YES.

IT'S SOMEONE ......WHO RECENTLY DIED.

...YOU SEE ANYTHING?

I'D LIKE TO WRAP THIS UP BEFORE THE POLICE ARRIVE...

THE BODY'S ALREADY BEEN CLEARED AWAY.

LOOKS LIKE THERE WAS A BIT OF TROUBLE HERE.

......

I CAN MAKE IT SO ONLY THOSE OF US HERE **CAN SEE HIM**, IF YOU WANT.

YES, PLEASE.

YES.

DO YOU HAVE SOMETHING YOU WANT TO ASK THIS SPIRIT?

ZUZUZU (FRSHHH)

ZU
(ZSHH)

LOOK AT YOU.

YOU'VE GROWN INTO A FINE MAN.

SHE'S NOT EVEN FAZED.

THOSE SIBLINGS ARE PREEETTY GOOD.

OH. HIS BRAIN STEM'S BEEN PIERCED RIGHT THROUGH.

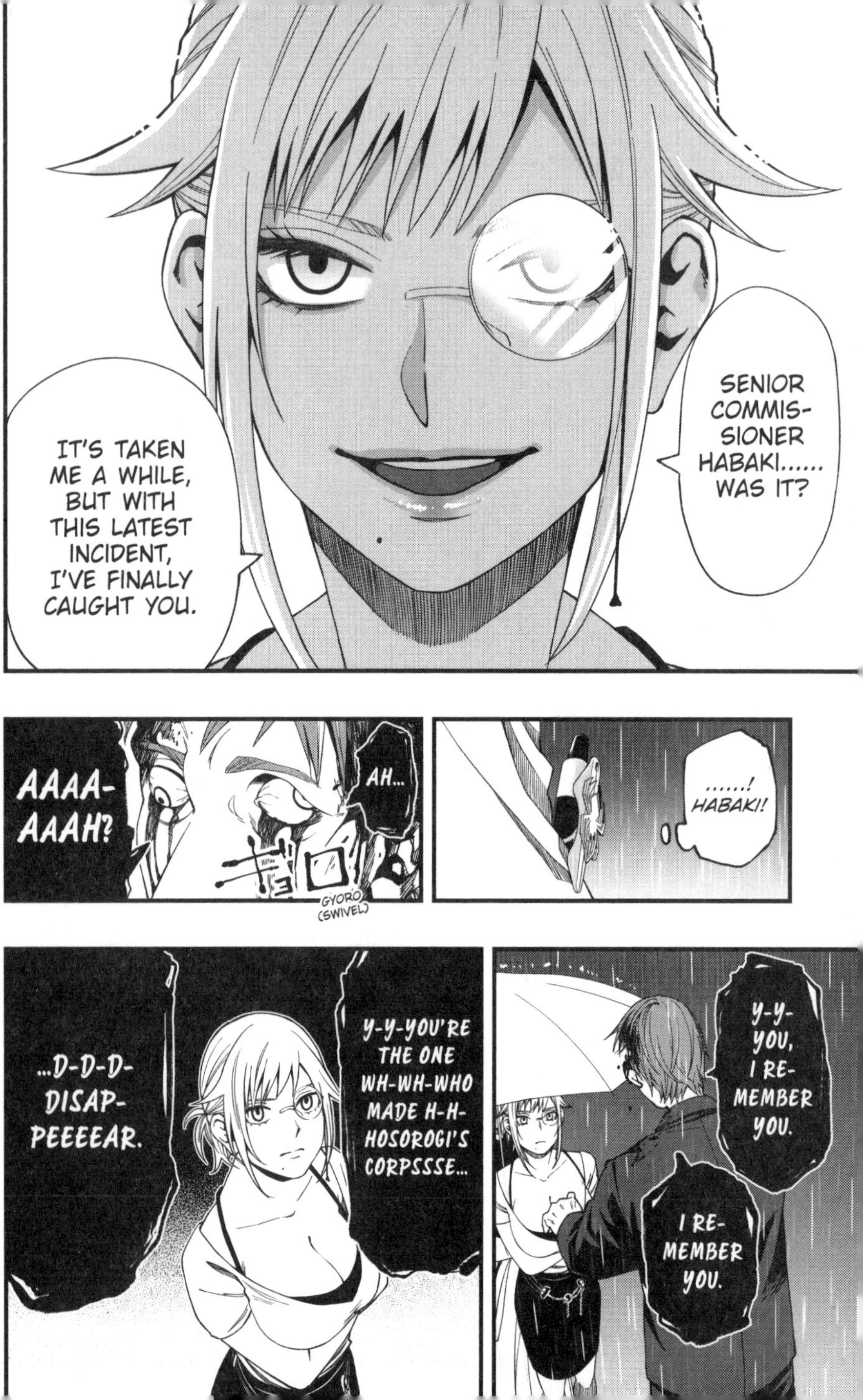
SENIOR COMMISSIONER HABAKI...... WAS IT?
IT'S TAKEN ME A WHILE, BUT WITH THIS LATEST INCIDENT, I'VE FINALLY CAUGHT YOU.
......! HABAKI!
AH...
AAAA-AAAH?
GYORO (SWIVEL)
Y-Y-YOU, I RE-MEMBER YOU.
I RE-MEMBER YOU.
Y-Y-YOU'RE THE ONE WH-WH-WHO MADE H-H-HOSOROGI'S CORPSSSE...
...D-D-D-DISAP-PEEEEAR.

YES.

I'M TERRIBLY SORRY ABOUT THAT.

HUH?

......

......

......

I KILLED HOSOROGI-SAN AFTER A LONG AND TUMULTUOUS AFFAIR...

...OR AT LEAST, THAT'S WHAT YOU WANTED IT TO LOOK LIKE.

BUT WHY IN A PLACE LIKE THIS...?

AND NOW YOU'RE DEAD!?

AND YOU FRAMED LISA FOR MY DEATH!?

HABAKI... YOU WERE ON THE SHORT LIST OF SUSPECTS, BUT STILL...

YOU KNOW WHAT KIND OF BUILDING THAT IS, DON'T YOU?

THERE ARE COUNTLESS WAYS TO MAKE A BODY DISAPPEAR.

S-sorry, I'll explain everything later.

THIS FEELS AWKWARD.

?

...

AFFAIR

AH!

I ONLY HAVE ONE QUESTION FOR YOU.

I'M NOT INTERESTED IN THE REASONS OR RESULTS OF KILLING HOSOROGI-SAN.

IF IT MEANS I'VE DEVIATED FROM YOU, THEN THAT'S THE HIGHEST COMPLIMENT.

OOOAAH...... I CAN'T BELIEVE YOU WOULD MAKE MINCEMEAT OF YOUR **LOVER'S CORPSE** WITHOUT ANY HESITATION... YOU DEVIANT.

YOU THINK...

...I'D... T-T-T-TELL.......?

WHO'S THE ONE WHO ISSUED THE ORDER TO HAVE HOSOROGI-SAN KILLED?

.... POLKA-KUN.

I'LL TELL YOU AS A SOUVENIR FROM THE NETHER-WOOOORLD.

YES.

THAT'S IT...

GI

GI

GI

OH...

OHHH!

GI (KRRK)

ALREADY ON IT.

IT'S A SPELL TO INDUCE A COMPLIANT STATE OF MIND.

IT'S A FAR CRY FROM BRAINWASHING, BUT I'VE TIPPED THE SCALES HEAVILY IN FAVOR OF HIS ABUNDANT EGO.

...WHAT DID YOU DO?

I HAVE SACRIFICED TO GET HERE.

SACRIFICED SO MUCH.

THAT'S RIGHT...

BUT I CAN'T BELIEVE THIS IS THE MAN WHO KILLED HOSOROGI-SAN......

TO THOSE CALLED "THE BASTARD CHILDREN OF SABARAMOND" ......!

OHHHH...... THAT POWER...

OHH...

IT...IT CAN'T BE. YOU'RE...

YOU'RE...

YOU KNOW ABOUT HIM...?

ABOUT SABARA-MOND......

......!!

HE'S...... BEEN LOOKING FOR ME!?

GUNE

OOOOH...! NOW HE'LL ACCEPT MEEEE!

THAT GREAT MAN WILL ACCEPT MEEEE ...!!

GUNE (WRIGGLE)

THE SORCERER... FROM THE "OTHER SIDE OF THE SKY"!!

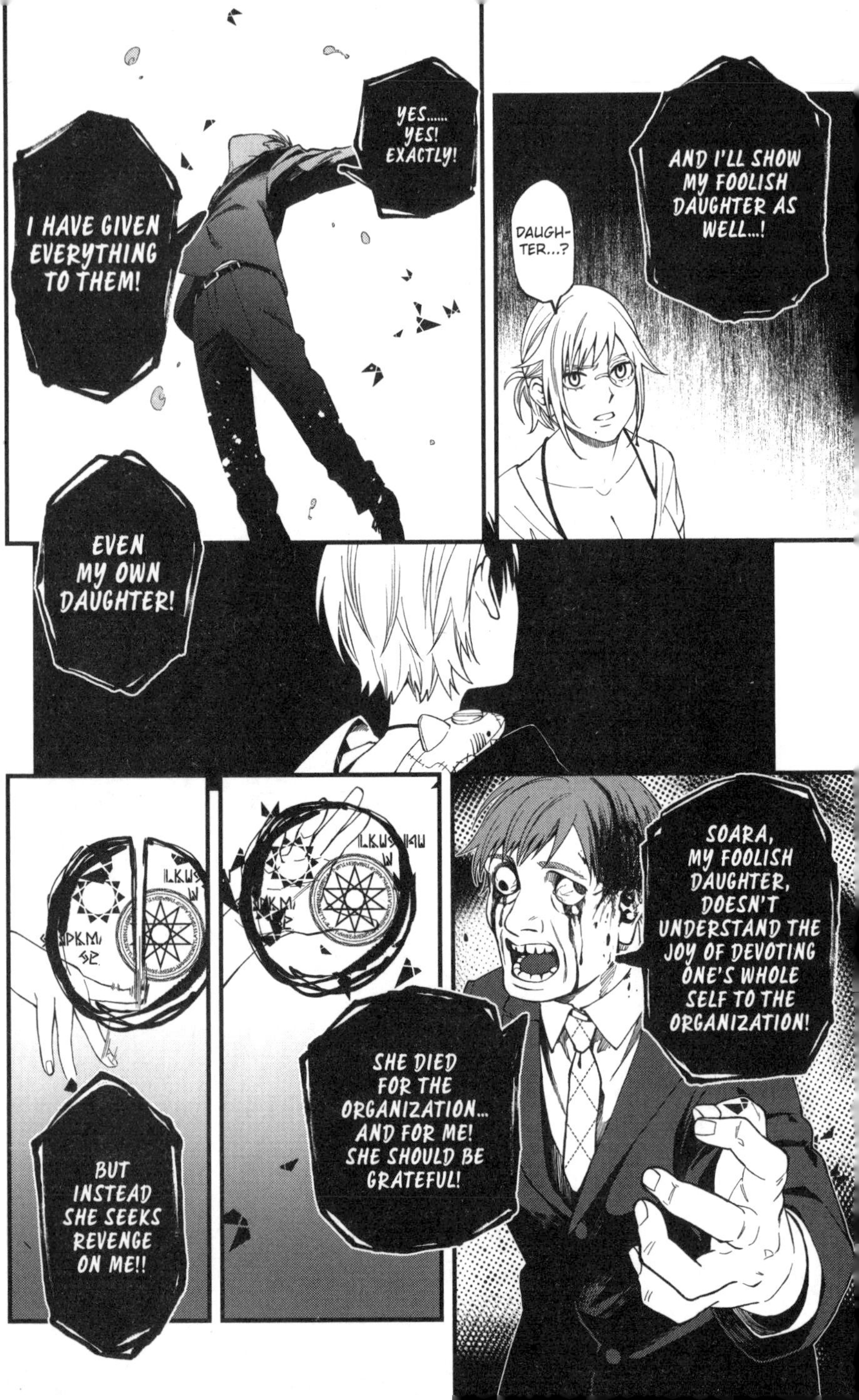
AND I'LL SHOW MY FOOLISH DAUGHTER AS WELL...!
DAUGHTER...?
YES...... YES! EXACTLY!
I HAVE GIVEN EVERYTHING TO THEM!
EVEN MY OWN DAUGHTER!
SOARA, MY FOOLISH DAUGHTER, DOESN'T UNDERSTAND THE JOY OF DEVOTING ONE'S WHOLE SELF TO THE ORGANIZATION!
SHE DIED FOR THE ORGANIZATION... AND FOR ME! SHE SHOULD BE GRATEFUL!
BUT INSTEAD SHE SEEKS REVENGE ON ME!!

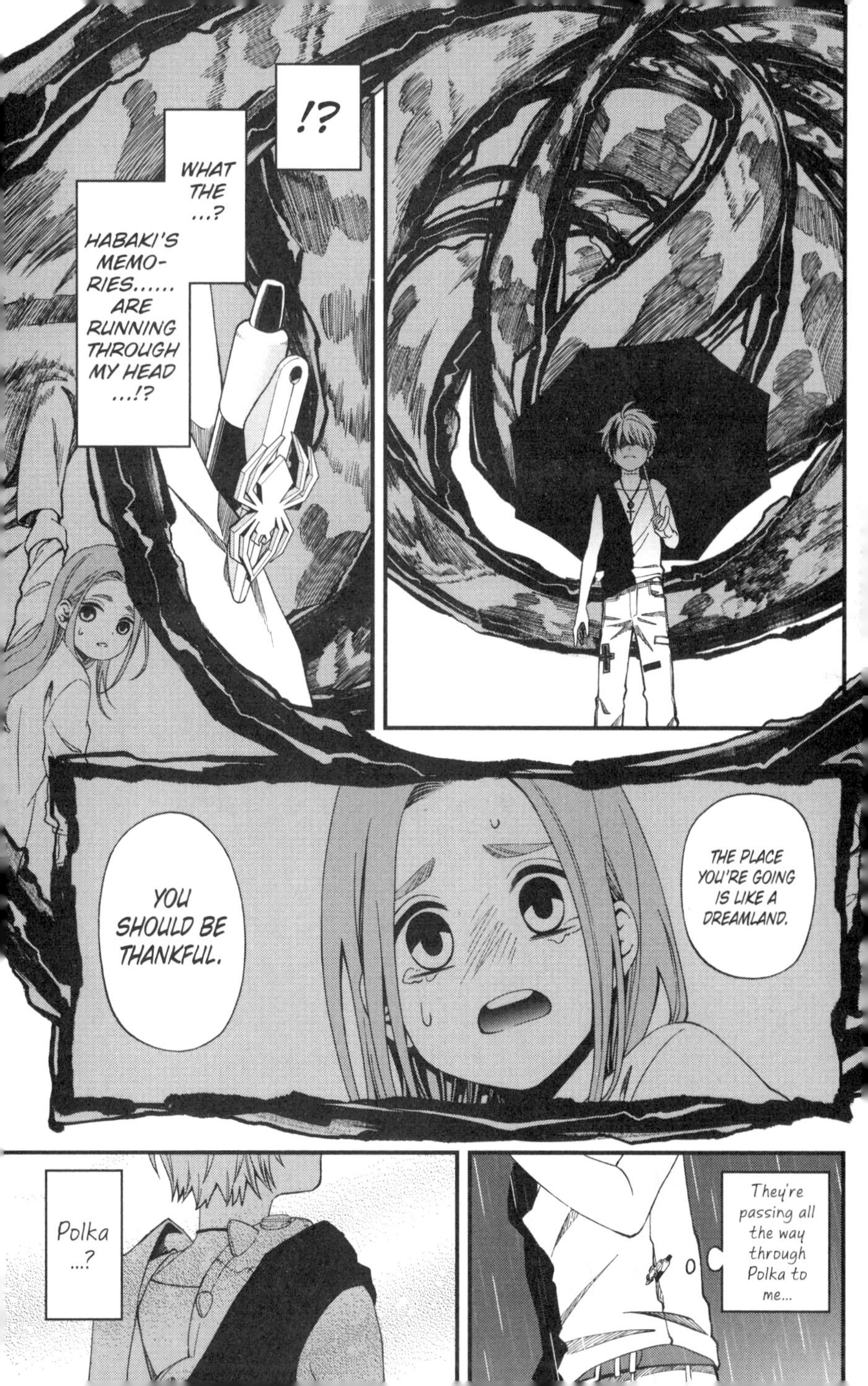
!?
WHAT THE ...?
HABAKI'S MEMO-RIES...... ARE RUNNING THROUGH MY HEAD ...!?
THE PLACE YOU'RE GOING IS LIKE A DREAMLAND.
YOU SHOULD BE THANKFUL.
They're passing all the way through Polka to me...
Polka ...?

SHOULDN'T YOU BE THANKFUL?

YOU'VE BEEN OF USE TO ME TO THE VERY END...

I SHOULD DRAW EVEN MORE INFORMATION FROM THAT MAN......

...I KNOW THAT'S WHAT I SHOULD DO. AND YET...

I AM *STILL* COMPOSED.

HUH? WHA...?

THIS IS...

ZU (CREEP)

CLA-RISSA-SAN.

ZU

ZU

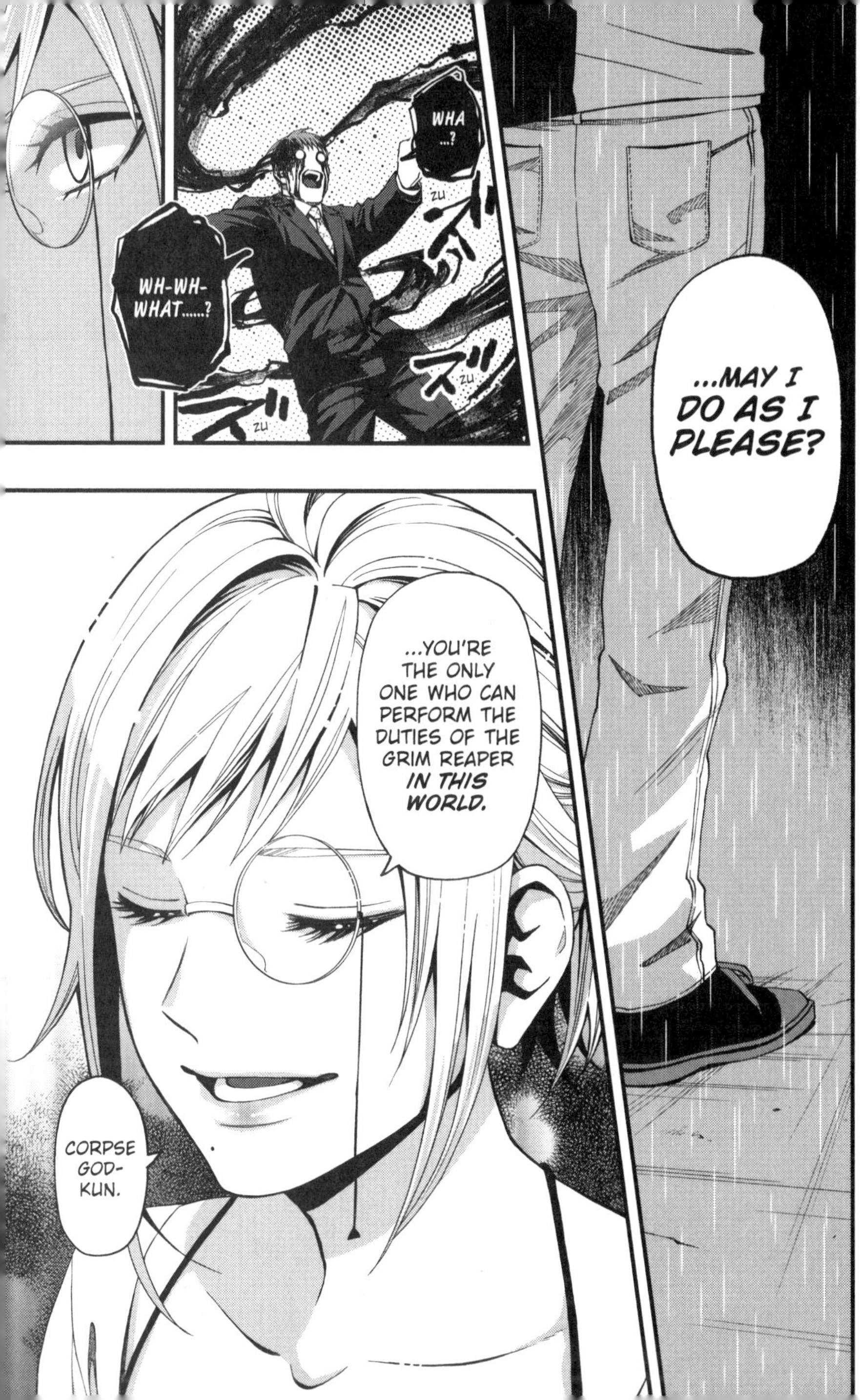

...MAY I DO AS I PLEASE?
WHA ...?
ZU
WH-WH-WHAT......?
ZU
ZU
...YOU'RE THE ONLY ONE WHO CAN PERFORM THE DUTIES OF THE GRIM REAPER IN THIS WORLD.
CORPSE GOD-KUN.

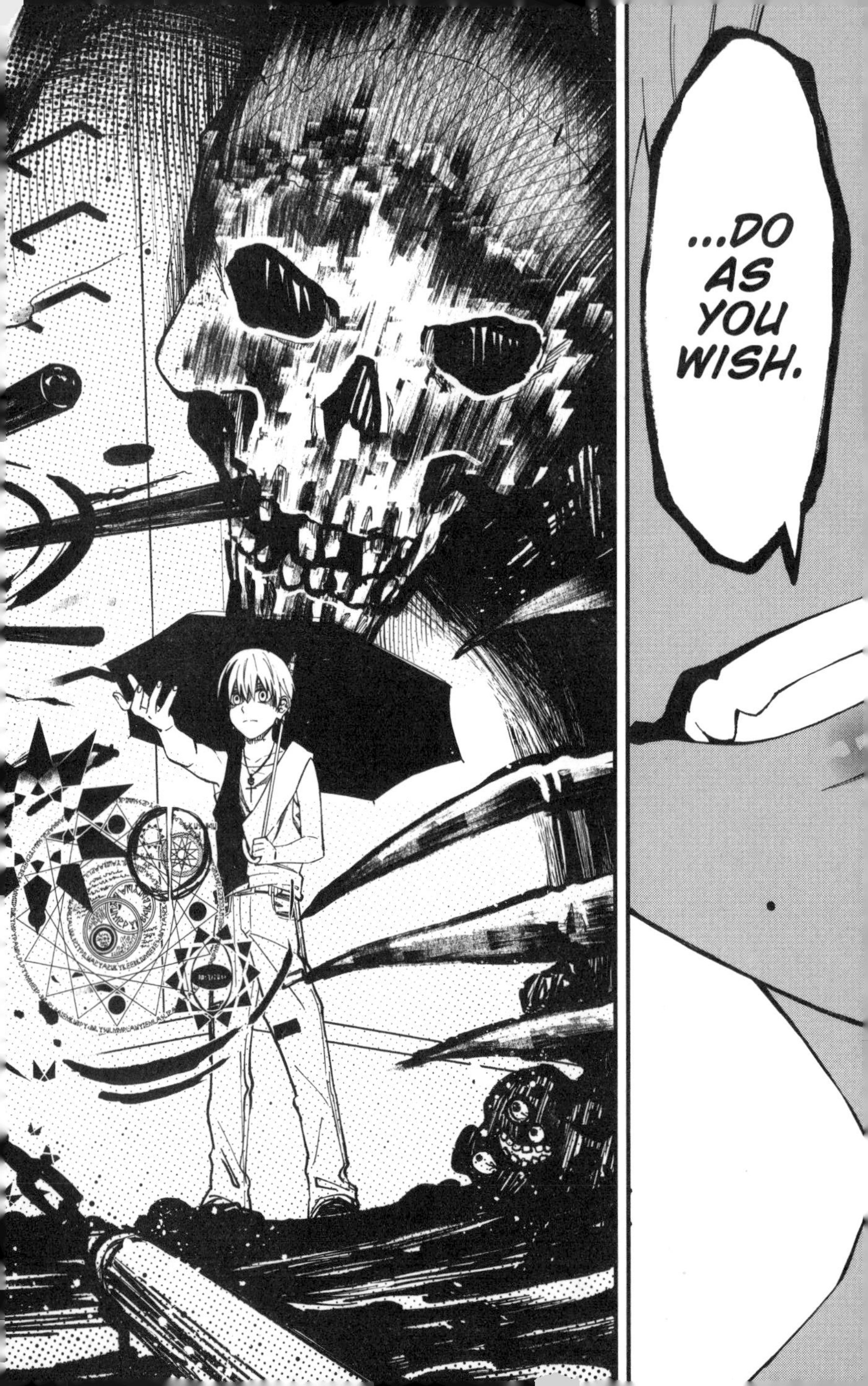
...DO AS YOU WISH.

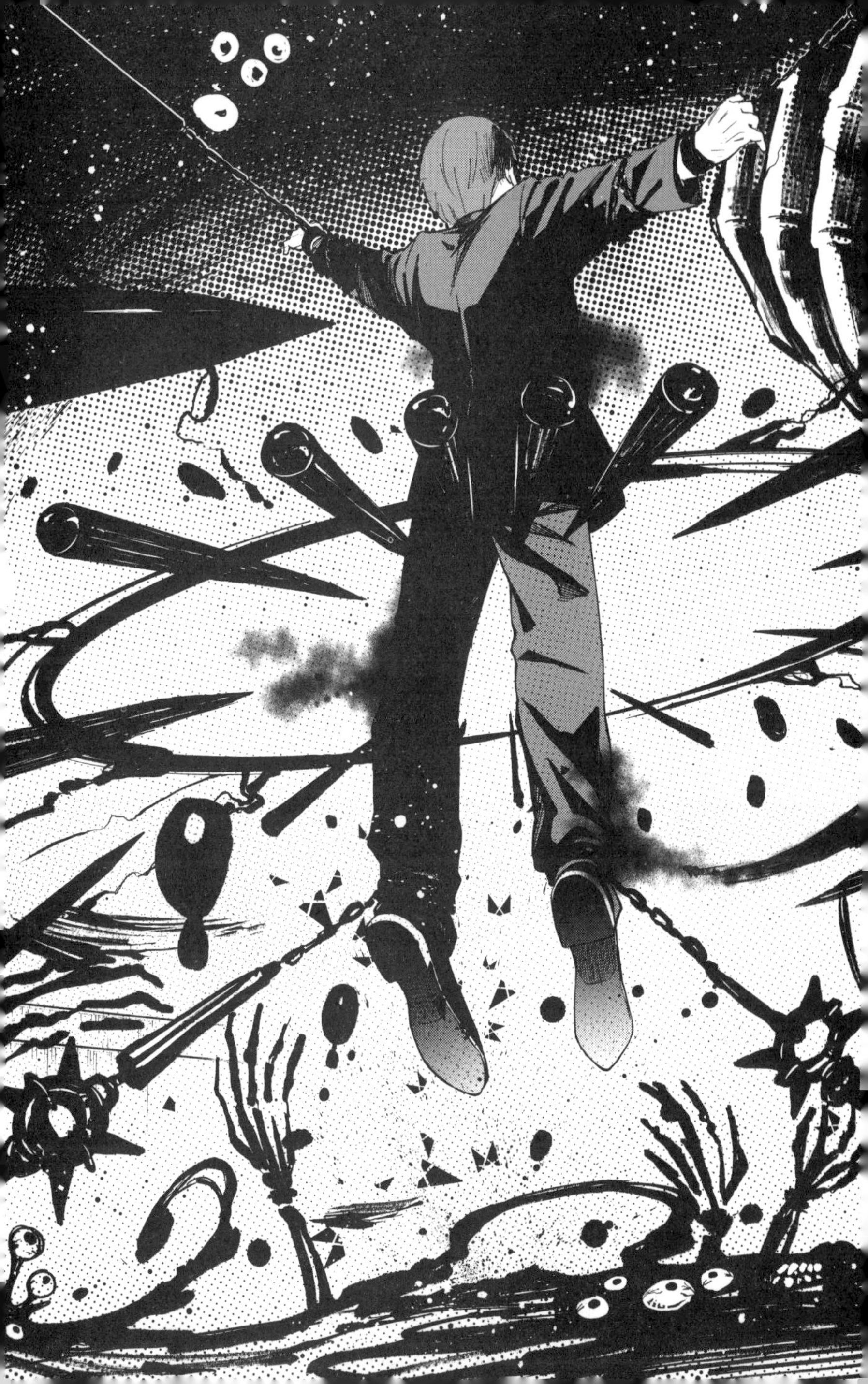

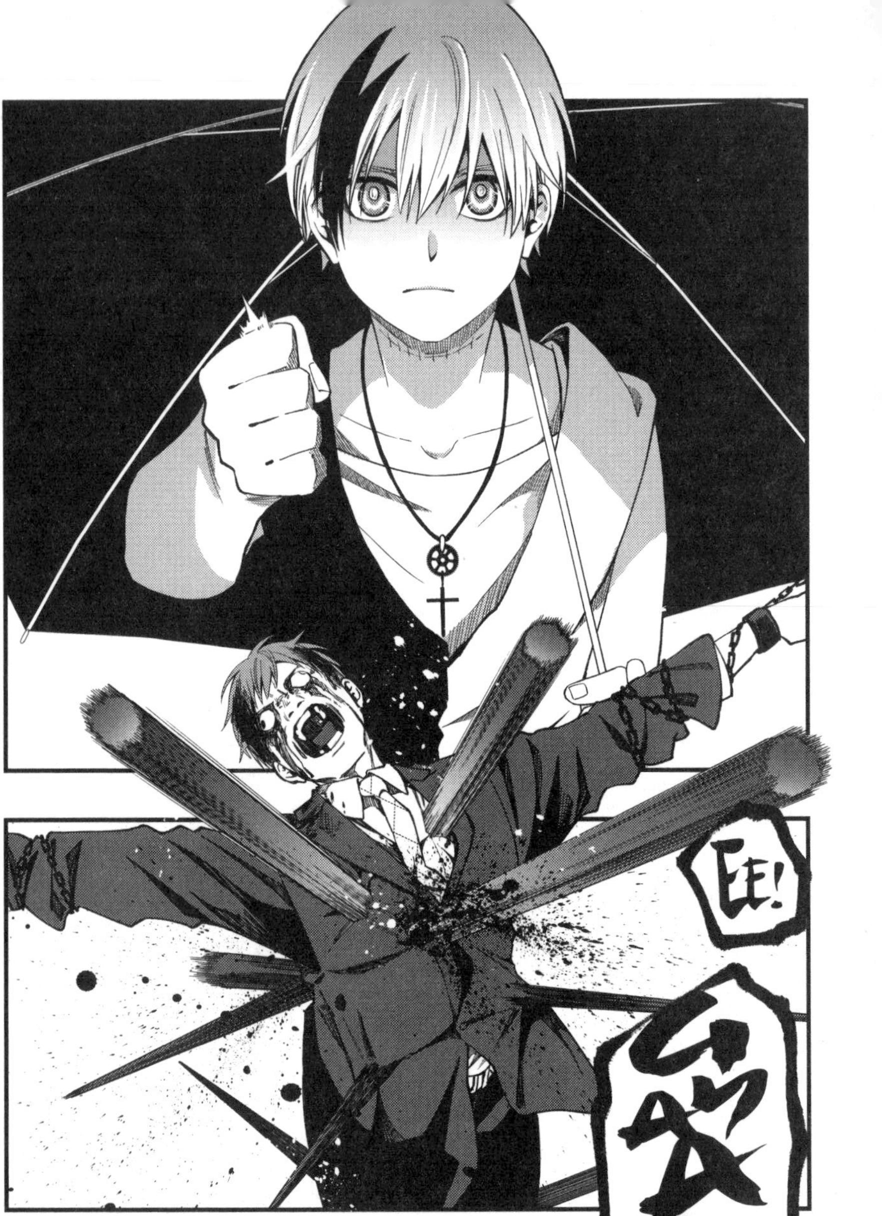
EE!

#56

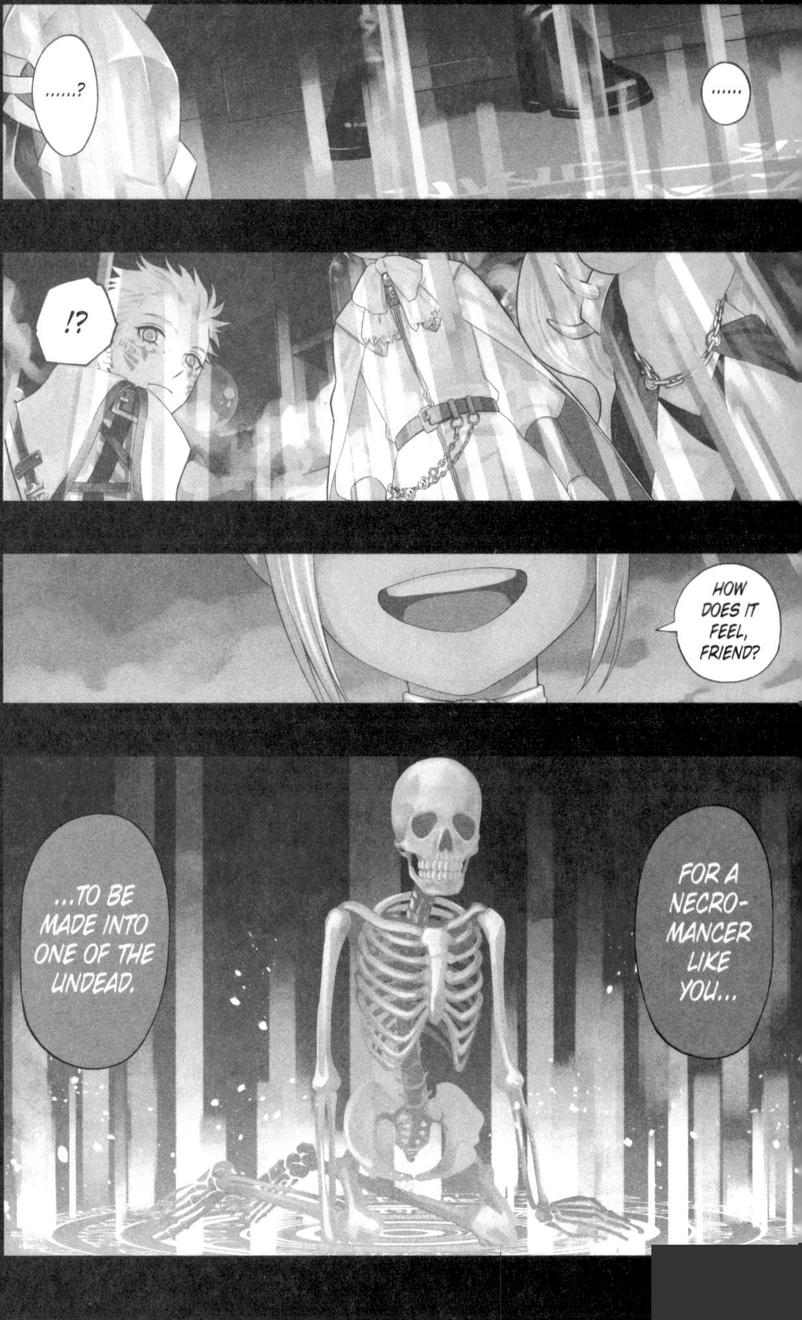
......
......?
!?
HOW DOES IT FEEL, FRIEND?
FOR A NECRO-MANCER LIKE YOU...
...TO BE MADE INTO ONE OF THE UNDEAD.

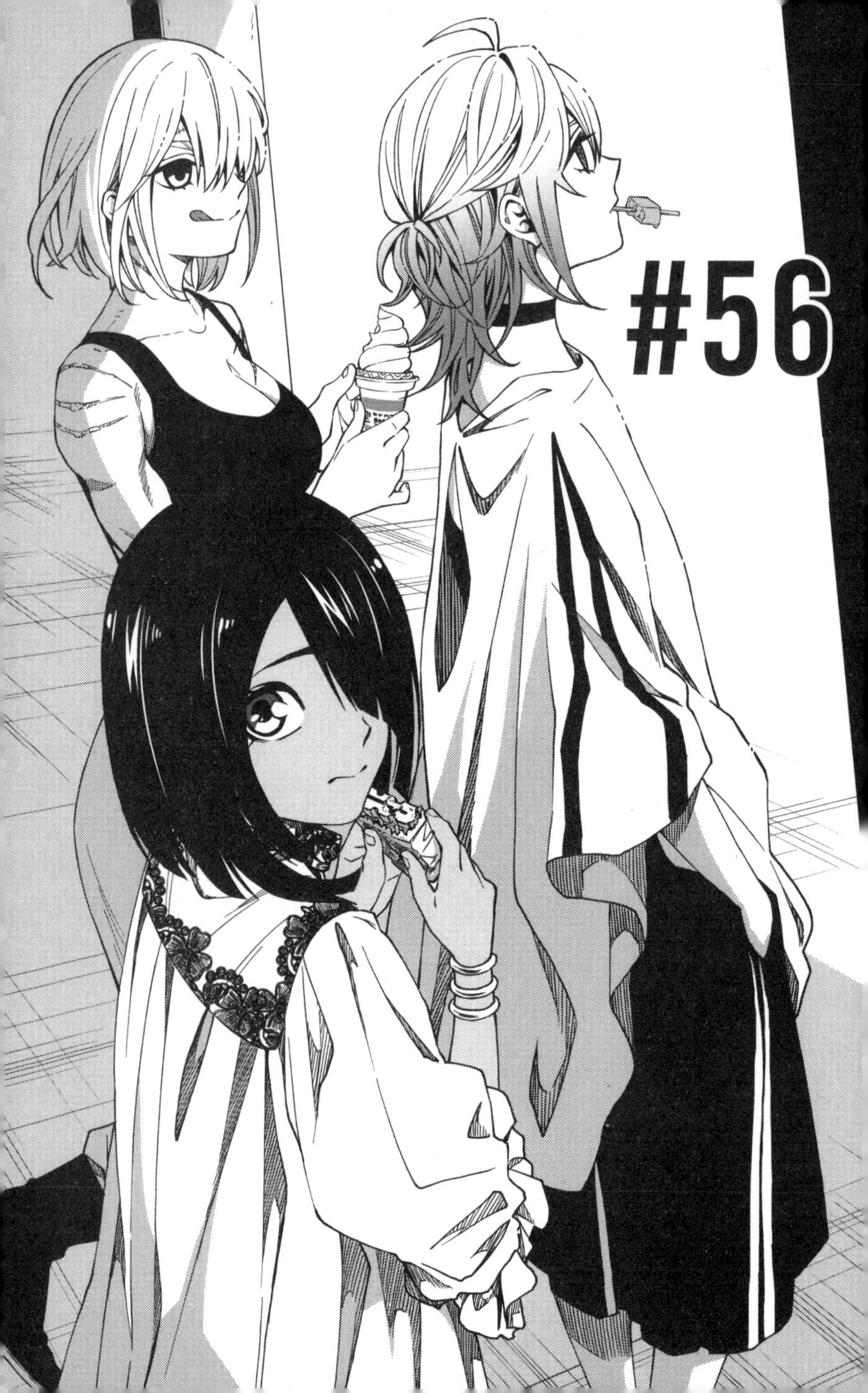
#56

HEY!
●●●●●!

HEY!

OH, I SEE. YOU'RE "THE GREAT CORPSE GOD" OF THE IMPERIAL COURT SORCERERS NOW, IS THAT IT?

......

YOU GONNA TREAT ME LIKE A STRANGER JUST BECAUSE I'M A COMMONER?

HEH HEH... WHAT GIVES?

I'VE HEARD ABOUT YOU, YOU KNOW?

YOU'RE A BIG SHOT IN THE EMPIRE NOW!

I WAS HOPING YOU COULD LEND ME A LITTLE MONEY.

ANYWAY. YOU KNOW WHY I CALLED YOU OUT HERE, DON'T YOU?

BECOMING A NECROMANCER'S A BIG DEAL.

APPRENTICED TO WANDERING BALCONY, ISN'T THAT RIGHT?

......!!

ギリ
GIRI
(GRIT)

I KNEW YOU WOULDN'T COME IF YOU KNEW IT WAS ME.

THAT'S WHY I USED MY OLD LADY'S NAME.

IT WASN'T EASY GETTING MY LETTER TO YOU.

THE LEAST YOU COULD DO IS PAY ME BACK FOR IT.

PASHI (SMACK)

I'M THE ONE WHO RAISED YOU AND INTRODUCED YOU TO THE EMPIRE.

...BUT YOU KNOW YOU'VE GOT ME TO THANK FOR IT, RIGHT?

THEY'VE BEEN HEAPING ACCOLADES ON YOU FOR WHAT YOU ACCOMPLISHED IN THE LAST WAR...

GI (GLARE)

C'MON.

N-NOW, NOW. DON'T BE MEAN.

EVEN IF YOU DON'T CARE ABOUT ME, DO IT FOR THEM. IT'D BE AWFUL IF THEY STARVED TO DEATH, RIGHT?

I'VE GOTTA FEED YOUR MOM AND LITTLE SISTERS TOO...OKAY?

DOSU
(SHUNK)

GIRI
(GRIT)

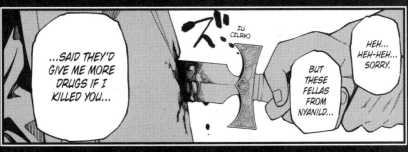

ZU
(ZLRK)

...SAID THEY'D GIVE ME MORE DRUGS IF I KILLED YOU...

BUT THESE FELLAS FROM NYANILD...

HEH... HEH-HEH... SORRY.

...WELL, NOT THAT YOU GOT ANY BUSINESS HOLDING A GRUDGE.

......!

DOSA
(THUD)

SO IF YOU'RE GONNA HOLD A GRUDGE AGAINST ANYONE, BLAME THOSE GUYS, 'KAY?

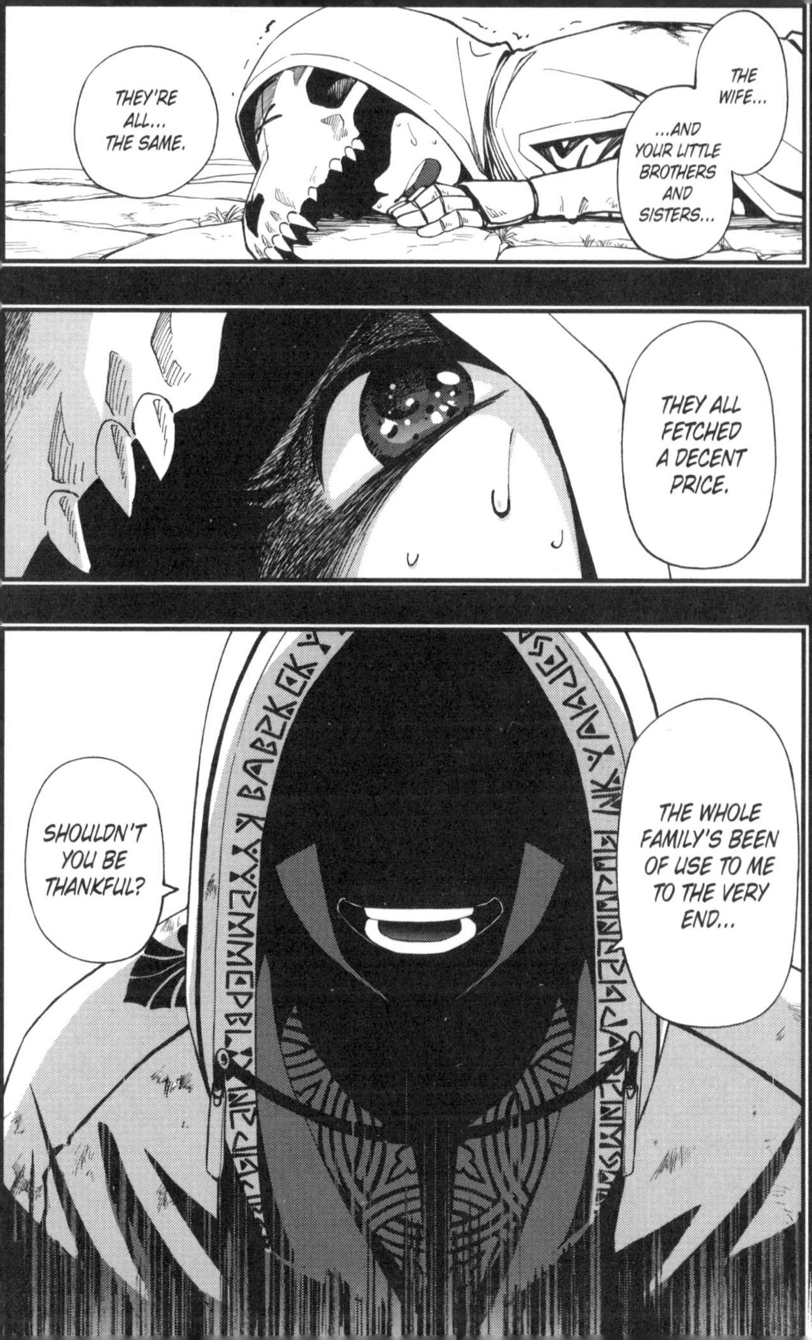
THE WIFE...
...AND YOUR LITTLE BROTHERS AND SISTERS...
THEY'RE ALL... THE SAME.
THEY ALL FETCHED A DECENT PRICE.
THE WHOLE FAMILY'S BEEN OF USE TO ME TO THE VERY END...
SHOULDN'T YOU BE THANKFUL?

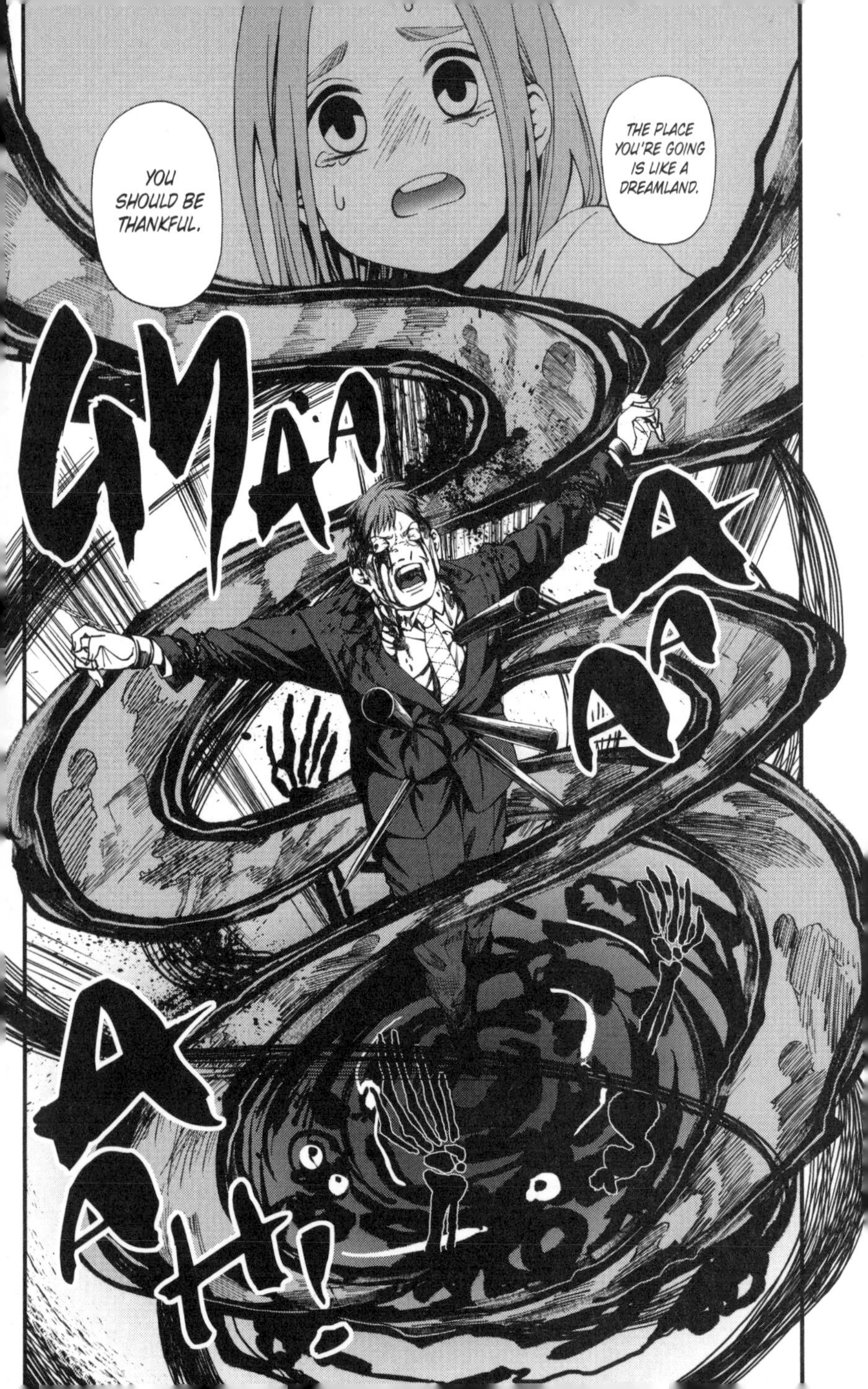
THE PLACE YOU'RE GOING IS LIKE A DREAMLAND.
YOU SHOULD BE THANKFUL.
GYAAAAAAAAH!

THERE ARE FRAGMENTS MIXED IN WITH HABAKI'S MEMORIES...

ARE THESE POLKA'S —

...NO... CORPSE GOD'S MEMORIES!?

HE'S DIRECTING HIS ANGER TOWARD HIS OWN FATHER ONTO HABAKI...

HE SAYS HE'S STILL COMPOSED, BUT HE'S OBVIOUSLY ON A RAMPAGE!

HE SEEMS *TOO CALM* FOR SOMEONE WHO'S LOST CONTROL.

...AND YET, SOMETHING FEELS OFF...

JUST WHAT IS IT THAT DRIVES YOU?

CORPSE GOD...

I EXPECT IT WAS PREPARED BY A CORRUPT HOLY WOMAN FROM THE GELDWOOD CULT.

IT WAS A CURSE DESIGNED TO DISSOLVE AND DESTROY THE BODY IN ORDER TO PREVENT IT FROM REVIVING.

...I KNOW I DID NOT RAISE YOUR SOUL TO BE SO WEAK AND FRAIL.

A TECHNIQUE TO DESTROY THE SOUL WAS ALSO APPLIED, BUT...

AND DO NOT FORGET THAT IT WAS ONLY ON A WHIM THAT I REVIVED YOU AS AN UNDEAD THIS ONE TIME.

STILL, I DO NOT BELIEVE THERE WILL BE A SECOND TIME.

THE NEXT TIME YOU THINK YOU WILL BE SEEING YOUR FAMILY, HAVE A BODYGUARD WITH YOU.

"HOW FORTUNATE I WAS ABLE TO MAKE HIS BRAIN INTO HIS SOUL CORE BEFORE IT WAS DESTROYED."

I REMEMBER YOU SAYING THAT WITH A HUGE SIGH OF RELIEF, IZLIZ.

HUH? IS MY MEMORY PLAYING TRICKS ON ME?

YOU SURE...?

PUI (SNUB)

YOUR MEMORY DECEIVES YOU.

BYANDY EMPIRE THIRD-RANKED IMPERIAL COURT SORCERER UTSUROJUZA

HE'S THE ONE WHO CURBED THE POISON AND THE CURSE THAT WAS ABOUT TO EAT AWAY HIS BRAIN, REMEMBER?

NIYA

NIYA (GRIN)

THEN AM I ALSO MISREMEMBERING WHEN YOU PLEADED WITH UTSUROJUZA?

YOU'RE JUST THE WORST, YOU KNOW THAT, YOU BEAUTIFUL OLD WITCH?

HA HA HA!

I THINK A MEDICINE MAN OUGHT TO EXAMINE YOU. PARTICULARLY YOUR HEAD.

YOUR MEMORY IS COMPLETELY MISTAKEN, YOUR HIGHNESS.

...I AM THE EMPEROR WHO RULES THEM ALL...

IN AN EMPIRE POPULATED BY ALL MANNER OF RACES...

...AND YET YOU'RE THE ONLY ONE WHO CALLS ME CRAZY.

RIGHT? DON'T YOU AGREE, CORPSE GOD?

BESH! (SMAK)

...BUT THEN YOU CALL HIS MAJESTY CRAZY? HOW AWFUL CAN YOU BE?

NOT ONLY DO YOU HAVE NO COMFORTING WORDS FOR YOUR APPRENTICE...

...IT'S TRUE THAT MY HEAD'S UNSTABLE AND COMING TO A BOIL.

I'M NOT CRAZY, BUT...

NOW, NOW, UTSURO-JUZA.

LET'S JUST LEAVE IT AT THAT.

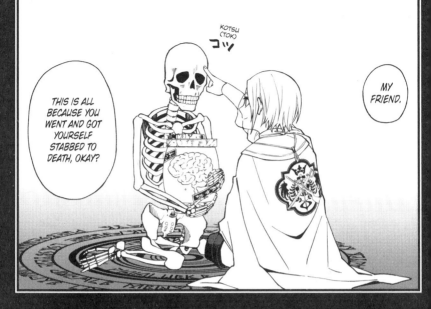

KOTSU
(TOK)
コツ

THIS IS ALL BECAUSE YOU WENT AND GOT YOURSELF STABBED TO DEATH, OKAY?

MY FRIEND.

STILL, I UNDER-STAND WHAT HE IS TRYING TO SAY.

...

IT WILL TAKE SOME TIME BEFORE HE CAN PRODUCE A VOICE FROM BONE.

HM? WHAT IS IT?

.......!

IT IS A GREAT SURPRISE TO HIM THAT, EVEN IN HIS NEW STATE, YOU TREAT HIM JUST AS YOU ALWAYS HAVE, YOUR HIGHNESS.

HE'S EVIDENTLY NOT GIVING SOMEONE ENOUGH CREDIT, THEN.

OH?

HE WAS UNDOUBTEDLY WORRIED THAT YOU WOULD CUT OFF ALL RELATIONS UPON SEEING HE HAS BECOME THE UNDEAD.

GYU (SQUEEZE)

I DIDN'T MEAN ME.

PEKO (BOW)

SHUN (GLOOM)

I MEANT YOU, ●●●●.

......

I LOOKED INTO THE MATTER.

THERE'S NO NEED FOR YOU TO SULLY YOURSELF WITH THAT LOWLIFE.

!!

AND DON'T GO THINKING ABOUT GETTING REVENGE ON YOUR DAD OR ANYTHING, OKAY?

NO MATTER WHAT BECOMES OF YOU...

DON'T FORGET, MY FRIEND.

...AND THE
EMPIRE
ITSELF...

...I....

...WILL
ALWAYS BE
ON YOUR
SIDE, OKAY?

AH...

BUCHI
(BLRCH)
ぶちぶち

BUCHI

WOOOW, THAT'S ROUGH...

.....

......

DON'T TRY TO ACT LIKE YOU'RE THE GRIM REAPER!!

...YOU'RE THE ONLY ONE WHO CAN PERFORM THE DUTIES OF THE GRIM REAPER IN THIS WORLD.

......

I BELIEVE THAT EVEN NOW.

GODS DON'T PLAY GAMES.

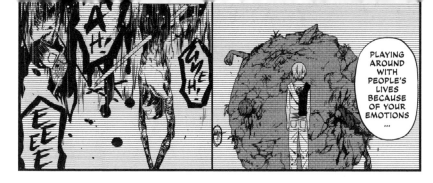

PLAYING AROUND WITH PEOPLE'S LIVES BECAUSE OF YOUR EMOTIONS ...

...MAKES YOU AS IMMATURE AS ME.

ZAWAWA (ZWSHHH)

グ" グ"... GUGU (STRAIN)

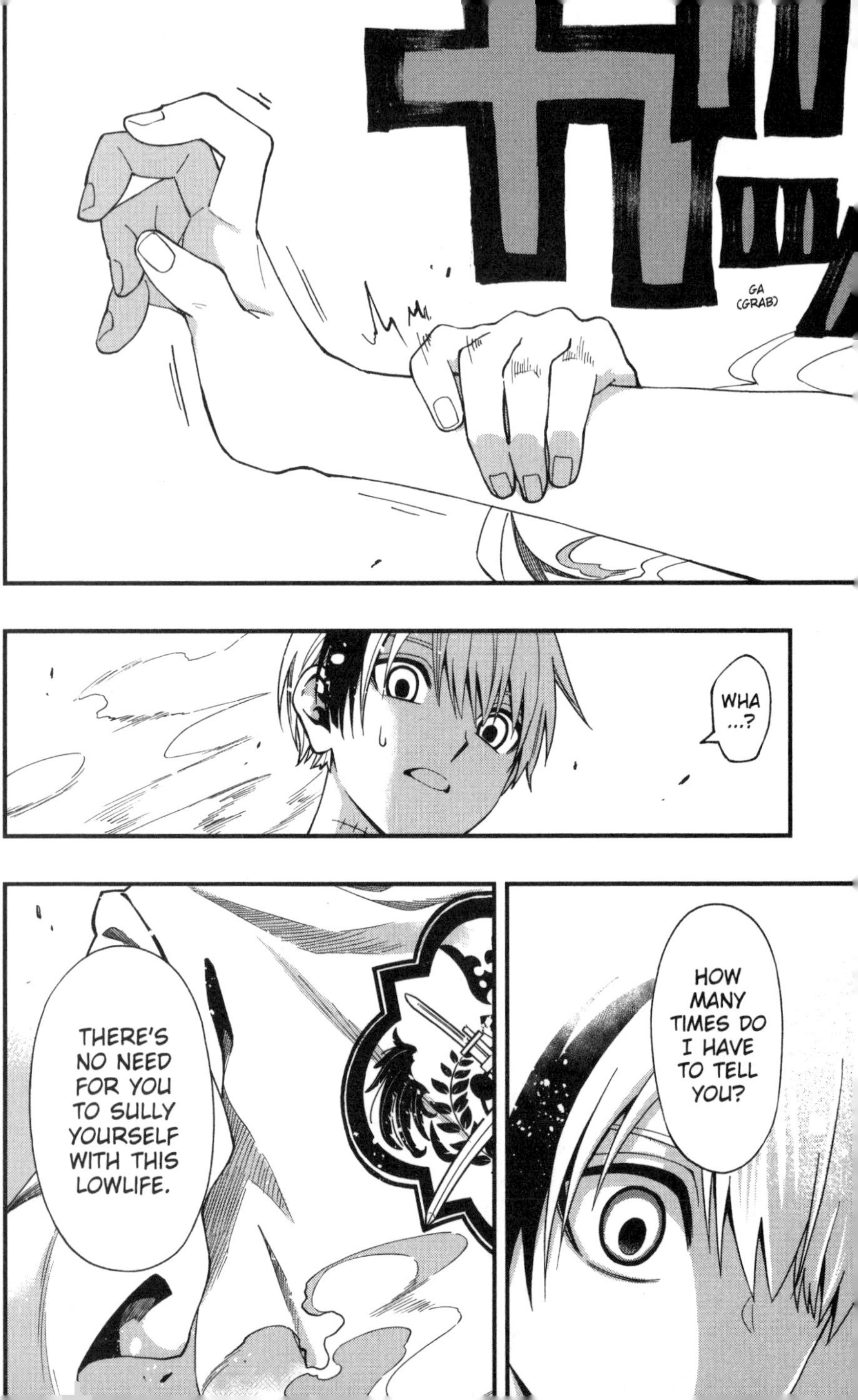

GA
(GRAB)
WHA...?
HOW MANY TIMES DO I HAVE TO TELL YOU?
THERE'S NO NEED FOR YOU TO SULLY YOURSELF WITH THIS LOWLIFE.

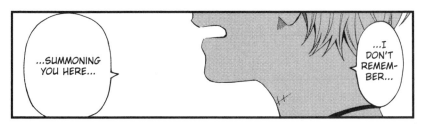

...SUMMONING YOU HERE...

...I DON'T REMEMBER...

...YOUR HIGHNESS...

DEAD MOUNT
DEATH PLAY

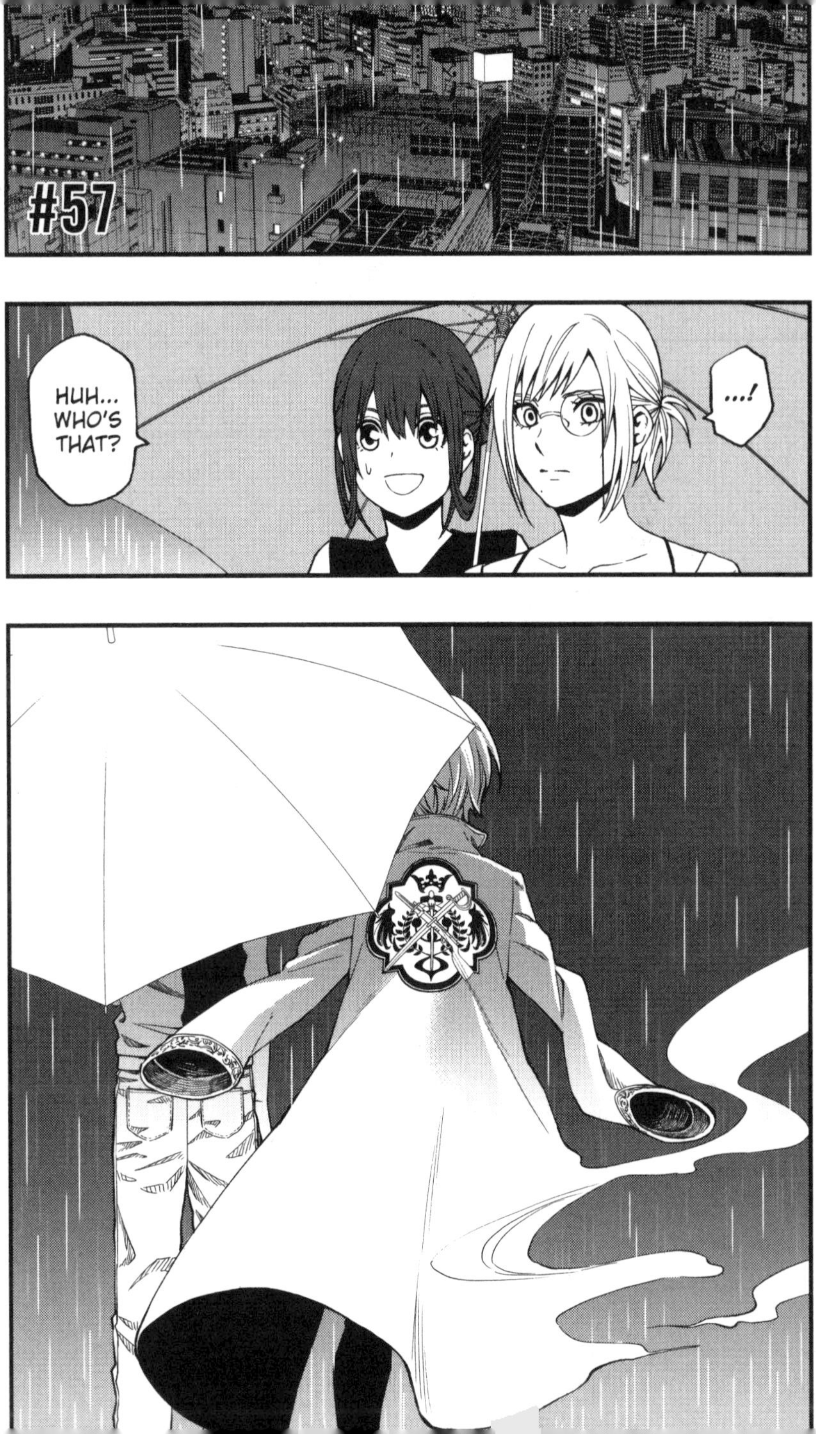
#57
...!
HUH... WHO'S THAT?

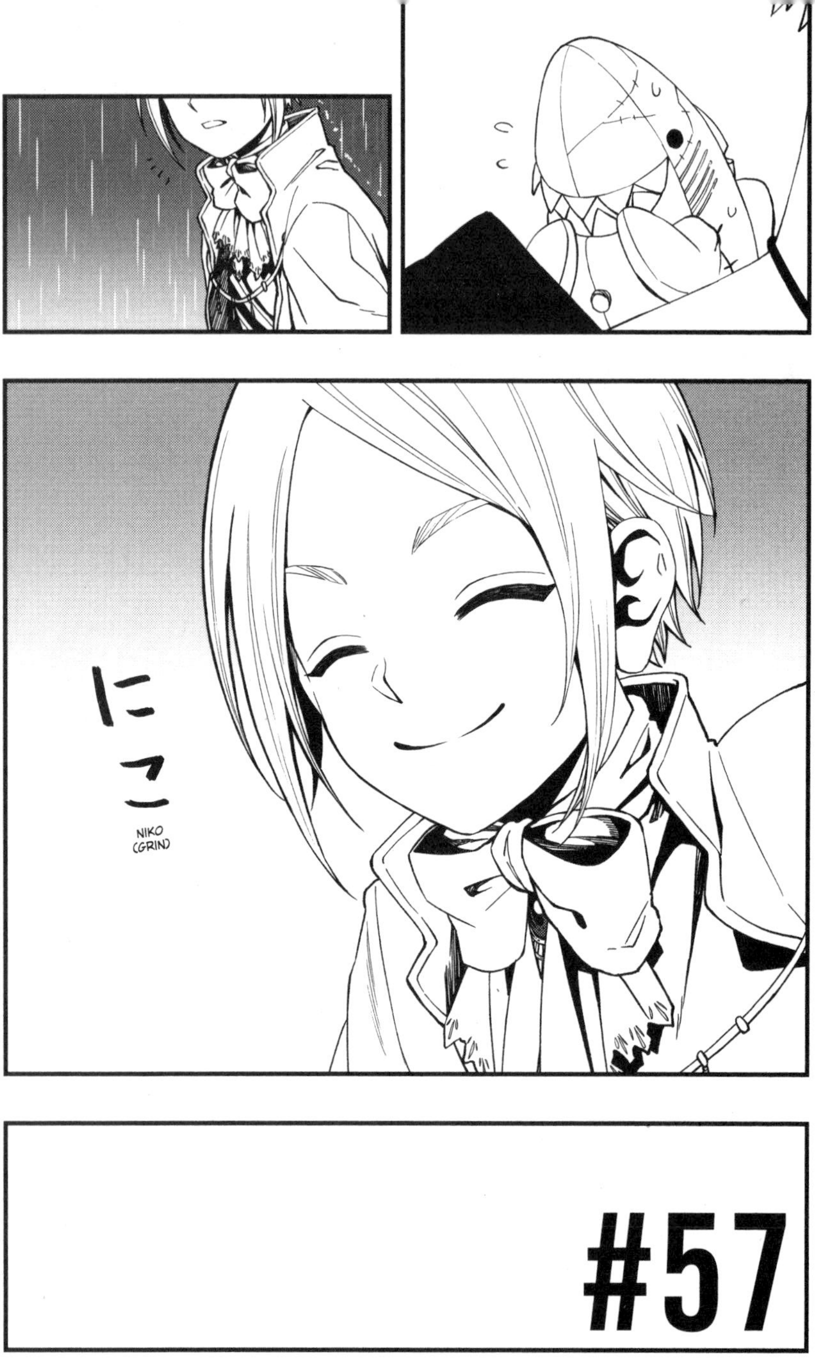
にこ
NIKO
(GRIN)

#57

OH! NOT AT ALL, LULU.

IS SOMETHING THE MATTER?

WHAT!? ...THAT'S THE DIRECTION WE JUST CAME FROM.

...FROM OVER THAT WAY?

I JUST HAD... A STRANGE FEELING IS ALL...

AFTER THE MESS A CERTAIN SOMEONE MADE IN THE BUILDING NEXT DOOR, THE POLICE ARE BOUND TO SHOW UP.

NO... WE'LL LEAVE THEM BE FOR NOW.

WHAT!?

WHAT DO WE DO NOW, BOSS? THINK WE SHOULD HEAD BACK?

HMPH...

HABAKI WASN'T COMPLETELY INCOMPETENT.

YOU DO REALIZE YOU DESTROYED THE BUILDING'S SCAFFOLDING THREE MINUTES IN?

BUT I THOUGHT YOU SAID I COULD DO WHATEVER I WANTED!

...THEN I THINK THEY'RE A FORMIDABLE OPPONENT WORTHY OF RESPECT.

PERSON-ALLY.

IF THE JAPANESE POLICE WERE ABLE TO CORNER SOMEONE LIKE HIM...

警視庁本部庁舎
Metropolitan Police Department Headquarters

東京都公安委
Tokyo Metropolitan
警視庁

...I'M SORRY.

AND SO... THAT'S THE SITU-ATION.

DON'T THINK YOU'LL BE GOING HOME FOR A WHILE.

BUT, IWA-SAN, IT'S NO LONGER JUST YOUR PROBLEM.

WELL... I DRAGGED YOU ALL INTO WHAT'S BASICALLY MY MESS......

WHAT ARE YOU APOLOGIZING FOR, MANAGER?

URK!

ALTHOUGH, I DO THINK YOU GOT A LITTLE TOO EMOTIONALLY INVESTED IN THE SITUATION WITH INSPECTOR HOSOROGI......

SHE'S RIGHT. THIS CONCERNS ALL OF US NOW.

GIVEN SOLITAIRE'S INVOLVED, THIS WAS ALWAYS UNDER THE JURISDICTION OF COMPS-3.

IT MIGHT BE BEST FOR YOU TO KEEP A LOW PROFILE FOR NOW.

MANAGER, YOU COULD BECOME THE TARGET OF REPORTERS YOURSELF.

...YATSU. POPS.

BESIDES, NOW THAT THE MEDIA'S GOTTEN A WHIFF OF THE HABAKI CASE, THIS IS GONNA GET BIG.

SORRY.

WE WEREN'T ABLE TO LOCATE HABAKI.

IF NOTHING ELSE, JUST DON'T LET YOUR GUARD DOWN.

...BUT WE DON'T KNOW THE SCOPE OR MAGNITUDE OF HIS ORGANIZATION.

I WANT TO SEIZE HIM BEFORE HE ESCAPES OVERSEAS OR SOME-THING...

THAT'S FINE. IT'S NOT LIKE WE CAN CHASE HIM DOWN WITH SO FEW PEOPLE.

LET'S JUST HOPE WE CAN END THIS BEFORE IT COMES TO THAT.

...YOU'RE RIGHT.

...SUMMONING YOU HERE.

...I DON'T REMEMBER...

BESIDES, I SHOOK OFF MY RESTRAINTS A *HUNDRED YEARS AGO.*

JUST COMING OUT HERE WAS TOUGH.

YOUR HIGH- NESS ...

PLEASE, DON'T BE SO COLD.

......

SU (SHF)

NOW IT'S YOUR TURN TO YIELD, OKAY?

I CAME HERE WITHOUT YOUR PERMISSION, NECROMANCER, SO I'LL BE GONE SOON ENOUGH.

RELAX.

ZURU
(ZLOOP)

...BUT HOW SPLENDID THAT I WAS ABLE TO REMEMBER THE WORDS FROM THIS SIDE THANKS TO YOU.

WHAT A CUTIE!

114

...I'M SORRY, BUT—

EVERYONE WANTS TO HAVE A FIRSTHAND LOOK.

THIS WORLD SEEMS LIKE A LOT OF FUN.

...UNTIL YOUR HEART WISHES IT SO.

IT'S FINE. I'LL WAIT PATIENTLY...

... SOME- DAY...

...FOR CER- TAIN.

...A FRIEND OF MINE......

WHO'S HE?

OR MAYBE... FROM EVEN BEYOND.

FROM THE OTHER WORLD...

...ALTHOUGH I'M NOT SURE WHEN IT COMES TO THIS WORLD.

YES. WE ARE.

......THAT'S RIGHT. I'D SAY WE'RE RATHER GOOD FRIENDS.

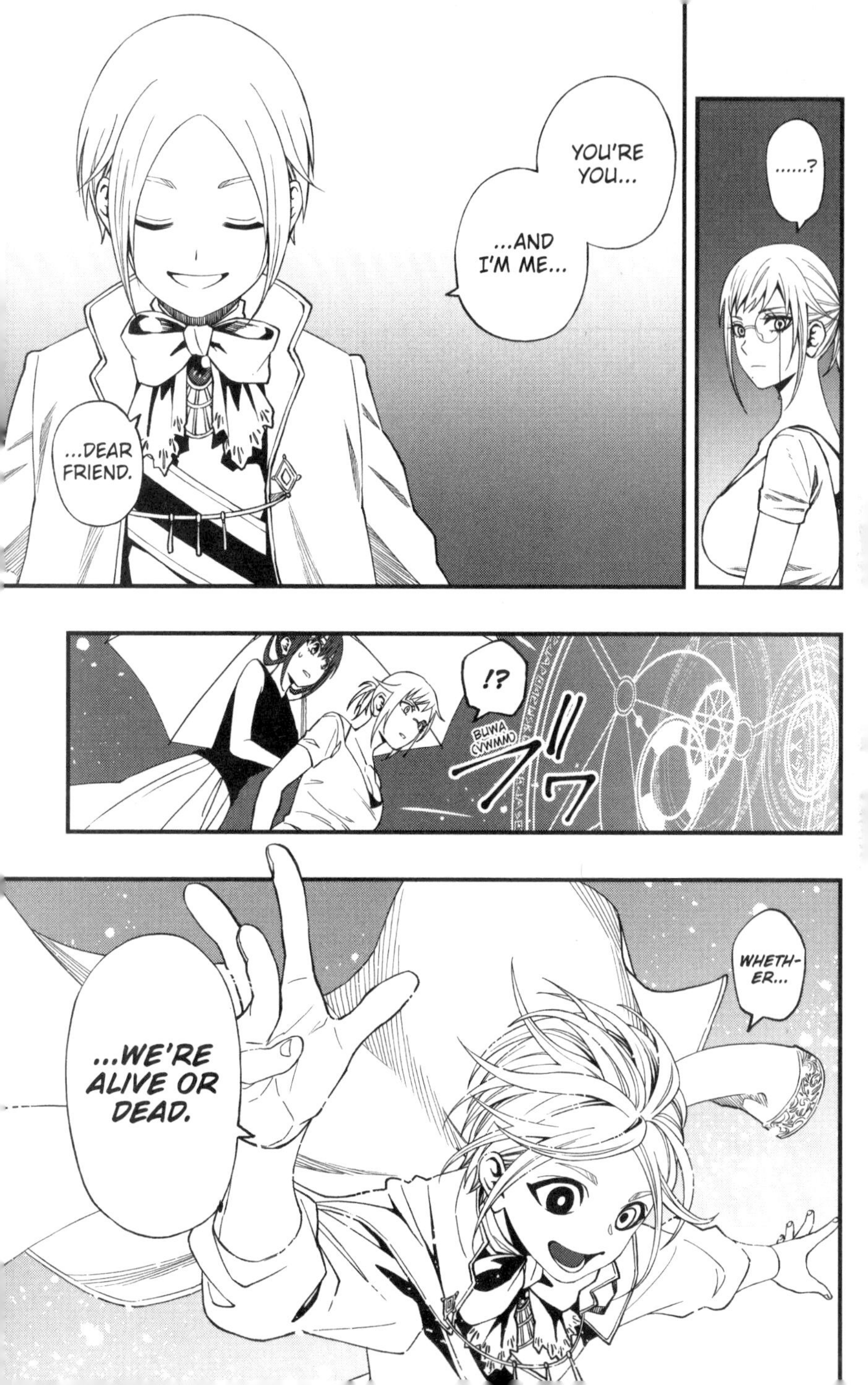
......?
YOU'RE YOU...
...AND I'M ME...
...DEAR FRIEND.
!?
BUWA (VWMM)
WHETH-ER...
...WE'RE ALIVE OR DEAD.

HM? ARE YOU WONDERING WHERE WE'RE GOING?

OH, I THINK YOU'LL ENJOY IT.

?

...BUT I DIDN'T MEAN YOU SHOULD RENOUNCE ALL HATRED AND BECOME A SAINT EITHER.

...LOOK. I KNOW I SAID NOT TO THINK OF REVENGE...

CALL IT ONE OF MY LITTLE INDULGENCES.

...THERE'S NO NEED FOR YOU TO GET YOUR HANDS DIRTY...

I SAID THIS BEFORE TOO, BUT...

...OVER SUCH A SMALL AND TRIVIAL THING—

STOP!! PLEASE! STOP!! PLEASE!!

PASH!
(SMACK)

......

IZLIZ.

DID YOU FORGET THE OLD LADY AND I WERE OPPOSED TO LETTING CORPSE GOD-KUN SEE THIS?

MICHI (SNAP)

BUCHI

AH!

BUCHI! (RIP)

BUCHI

THIS POOR EXCUSE FOR A FATHER... I THOUGHT I MIGHT DO AWAY WITH HIM AND NOT LEAVE A TRACE.

GH...

F...

FORGIVE MEEE—

GWAAA!

I'M SO SORRY...

...I....I'M SORRY...

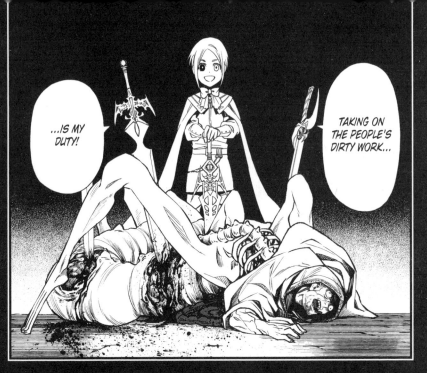

...IS MY DUTY!

TAKING ON THE PEOPLE'S DIRTY WORK...

SO...

...THERE'S NO NEED FOR YOU TO GET YOUR HANDS DIRTY...MY DEAR FRIEND.

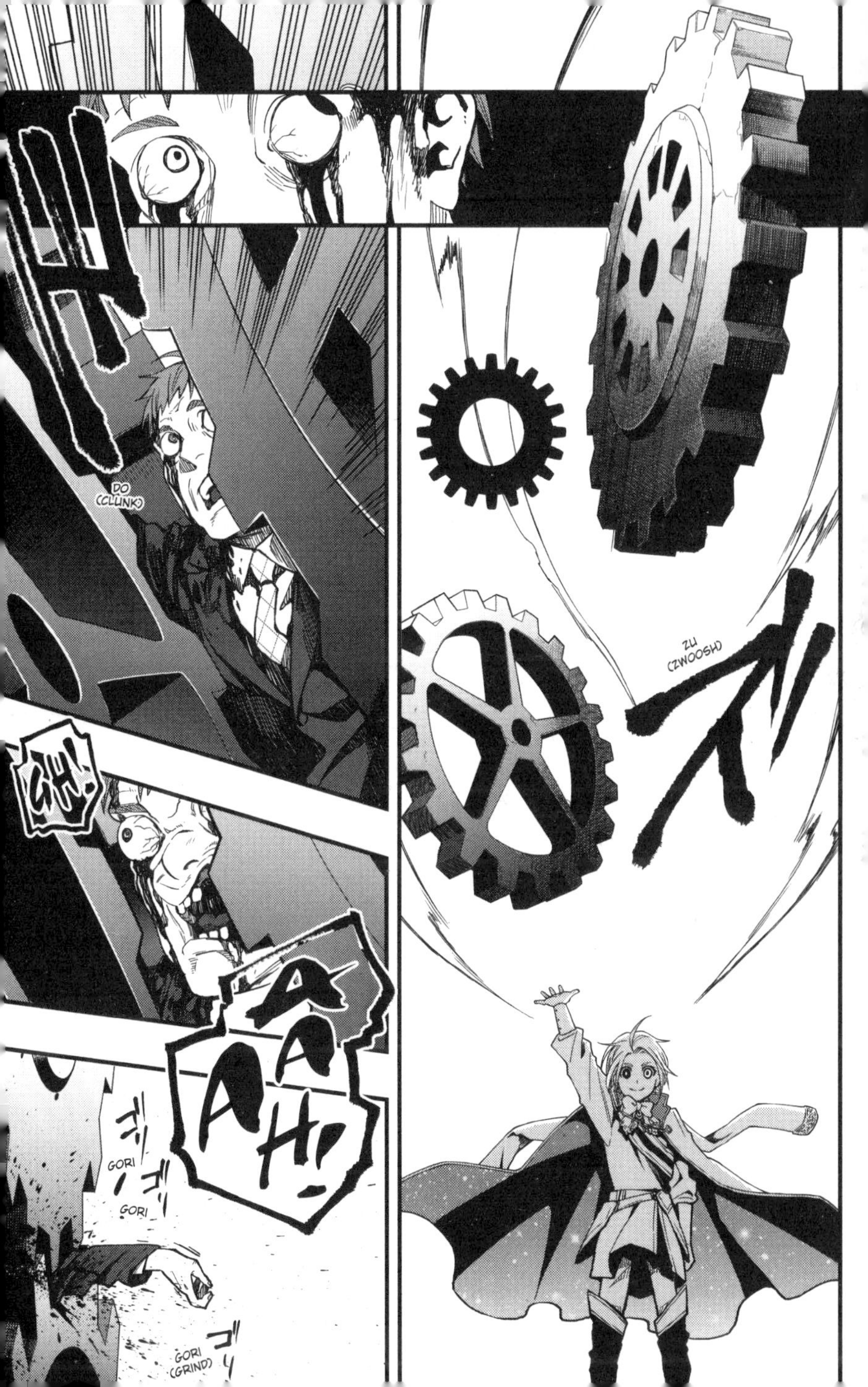
ZU
(ZWOOSH)
DO
(CLUNK)
GH!
AAAH!
GORI
GORI
GORI
(GRIND)

BICHA
(SPLIT)
ビ

チャ

SUCH CONCEITED THINKING IS...

...WHAT GOT YOU ASSASSI-NATED...

...YOUR HIGH-NESS.

...MAYBE SO.

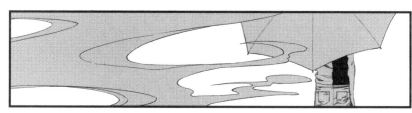

I'D PLANNED TO WAIT AND SEE WHAT WOULD HAPPEN, BUT...

...I GUESS I'LL START TOMORROW.

SO... HE'S DISAPPEARED.

WE'VE GOT THE BUG AND MY COMRADE FROM BACK HOME...

WHICH SHOULD I PRIORITIZE FIRST?

THIS CITY'S ABSOLUTELY CRAWLING WITH TROUBLE-MAKERS.

THIS IS ABOUT A WORLD THAT DOESN'T CONCERN US.

JUST LEAVE IT BE.

WHAT DO WE DO?

...MY WISH REMAINS THE SAME AS IT WAS BEFORE, YOUR HIGHNESS.

I WISH FOR A WORLD WHERE EVERYONE CAN LIVE IN PEACE.

A WORLD WHERE...... YOU DON'T HAVE TO GET YOUR HANDS DIRTY.

THAT'S WHY...

...I HAVE TO VENTURE EVEN DEEPER.

UMBRELLAS: WATCH OUT FOR FIRES

...WHICH ARE BLENDING INTO THIS ONE.

INTO THE SHADOWS OF THAT WORLD...

...it's extremely sloppy to say the name of your contact over the phone like that.

Senior Commissioner Habaki.

BU (CLICK)

...AHH.

IS THAT THE END OF THE LINE FOR HABAKI-SAN?

#58

PUSHUU (CHHSH)

IF THINGS GO SOUTH, I'M A GONER.

I JUST HOPE THE HIGHER-UPS CAN DISPOSE OF HIM BEFORE HE SPILLS ANYTHING ABOUT ME.

I'LL HAVE TO LOSE THIS PHONE SOMEWHERE IN THE NEXT FEW HOURS—

SHOULD I GO INTO HIDING FOR A WHILE...?

GASHA (CLATTER)

HOT ....!

PORO (DROP)

JIRI (SIZZL)

タ た タ タ タ
(TAP)
TA TA TA
TA
TA
TA
TA
TA

YES.

SORRY ABOUT THAT...

YOU DROPPED THIS.

OH DEAR.

HEY...

EXCUSE ME!?

ガシ (GRAB)

HUH...?

タ た タ タ タ
た タ
TA TA TA
TA
TA
TA た
タ た
TA
TA
TA
た
タ た
TA
TA
TA
た
TA

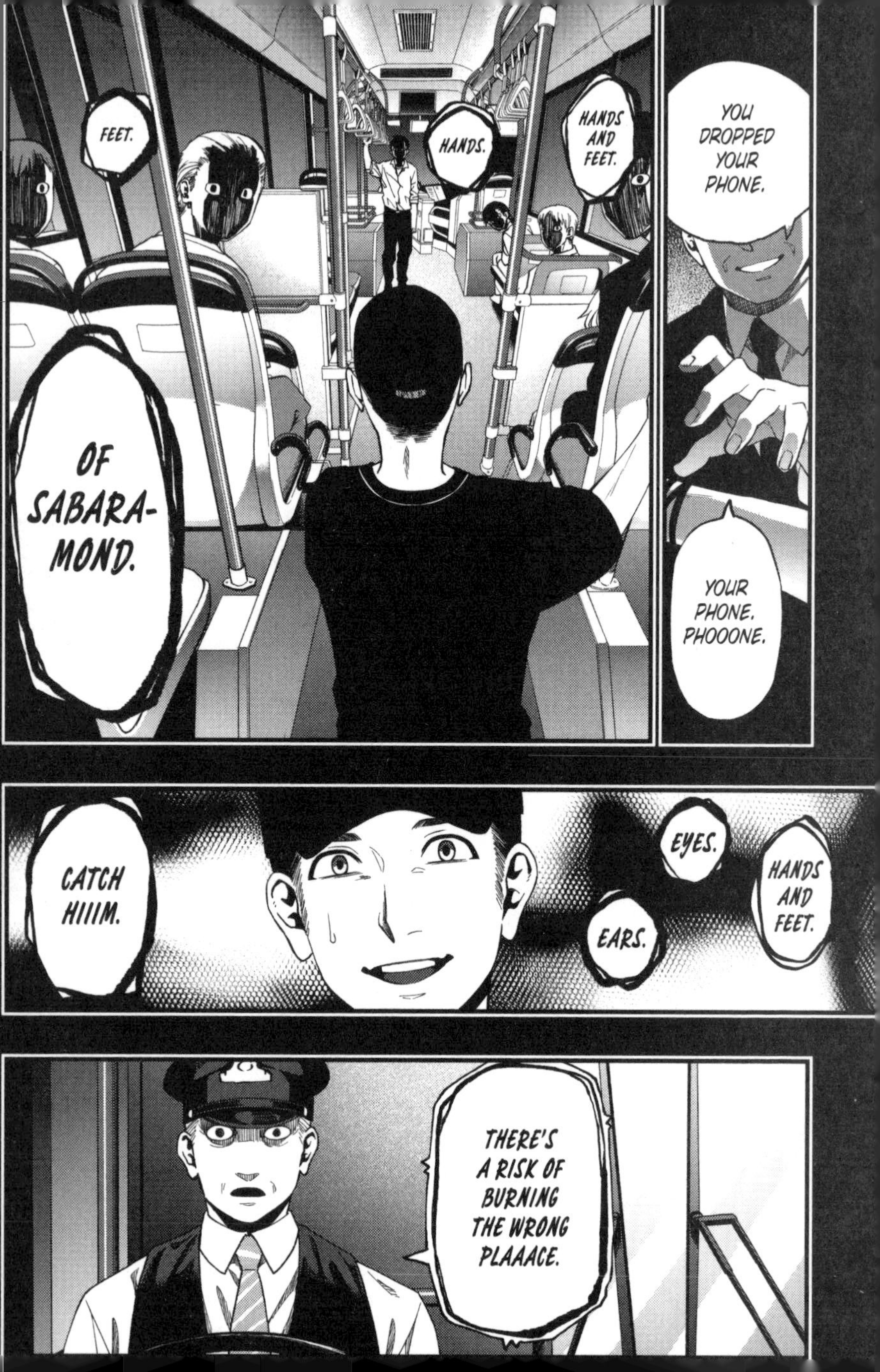
YOU DROPPED YOUR PHONE.
YOUR PHONE. PHOOONE.
HANDS AND FEET.
HANDS.
FEET.
OF SABARA-MOND.
HANDS AND FEET.
EYES.
EARS.
CATCH HIIIM.
THERE'S A RISK OF BURNING THE WRONG PLAAACE.

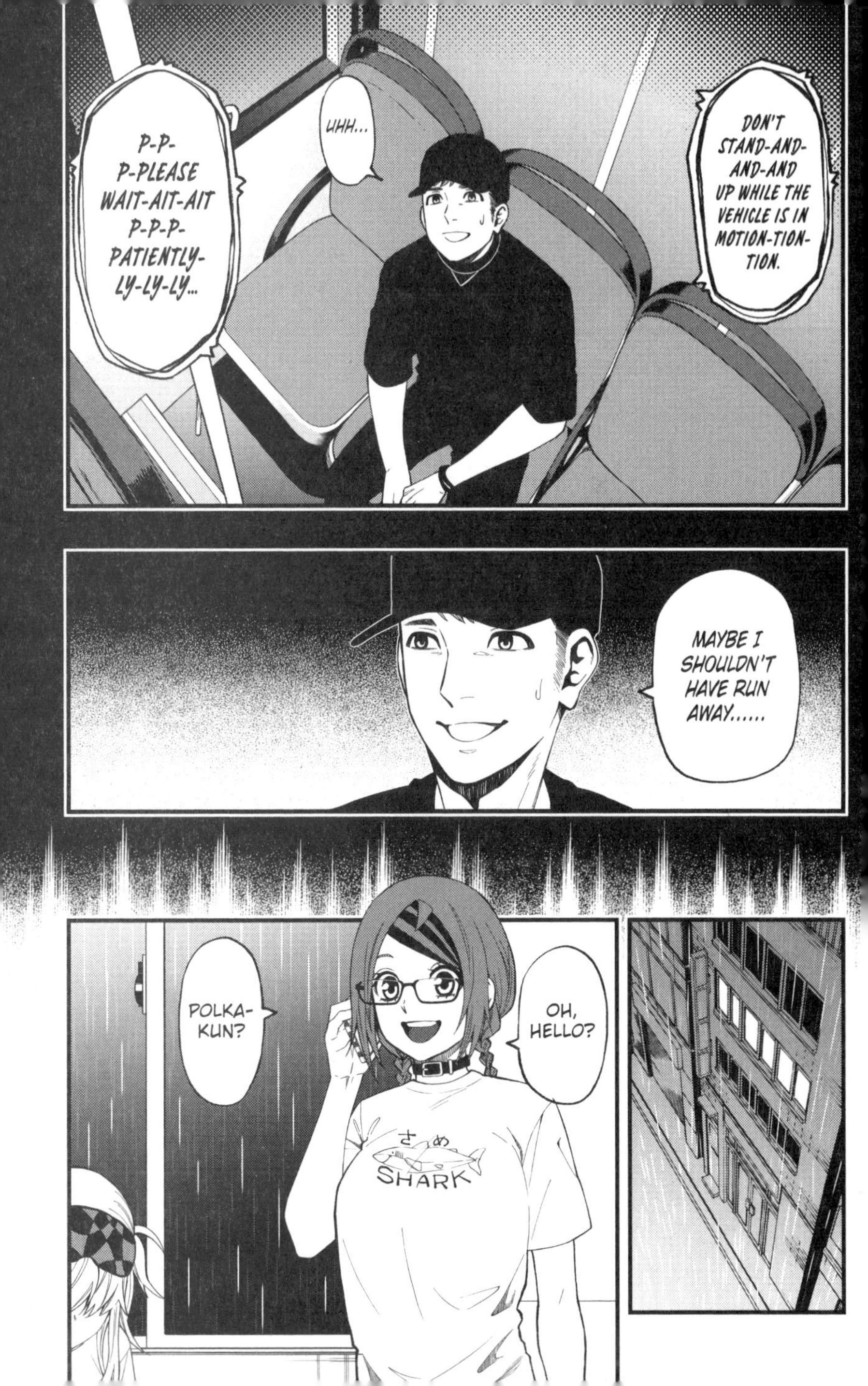
DON'T STAND-AND-AND-AND UP WHILE THE VEHICLE IS IN MOTION-TION-TION.
UHH...
P-P-P-PLEASE WAIT-AIT-AIT P-P-P-PATIENTLY-LY-LY-LY...
MAYBE I SHOULDN'T HAVE RUN AWAY......
OH, HELLO?
POLKA-KUN?
さめ
SHARK

Huh? Yeah, I'm fine.

I'm with Clarissa-san right now.

WE'RE BACK. EVERYTHING OKAY WITH YOU?

......

FOR NOW.

WILL PACKING TAPE DO?

UM...... AREN'T YOU SURPRISED?

......

THIS SURE IS WELL MADE.

134

I-I SEE...

I'VE ASKED THEM TO CREATE A SHARK ROBOT BEFORE.

ABOUT WHAT?

THIS IS SHINOYAMA COMPANY TECH, RIGHT?

BE-SIDES...

...I ALWAYS KNEW YOU WERE KEEPING AT LEAST ONE OR TWO SECRETS FROM ME, XIAOYU-KUN.

BIRI (PEEL)

ビリ

EVEN IF YOU CAN'T TELL ME YOUR SECRETS, THERE ARE STILL SOME THINGS I KNOW.

PETA (STICK)

ペタ

NO. THANK YOU...!

BOSS!

I MEAN, IF YOU COULD TRANSFORM INTO A TINY SHARK OR SOMETHING, THEN I'D DEFINITELY BE SURPRISED, AND I'D PROBABLY ASK YOU TO MARRY ME.

NO...

PON
(PAT)
ぽん

PON
ぽん

AH...

THANK YOU.

POSU
(POMF)
ぽす

I KNOW YOU WORKED HARD TO PROTECT US.

KURU-PON.

I ONLY ACTED...

...FOR MY OWN BENEFIT...

AH...

I HEARD WHAT HAP-PENED.

THE INJURY ON YOUR LEG... IS IT SOMETHING YOU CAN EXPLAIN AWAY TO A DOCTOR?

HELLO, TAKUMI-KUN?

HEE HEH HYA!

AND IF I TOLD A DOCTOR I DID IT TO MYSELF, I IMAGINE THEY'D SUSPECT I'M A JUNKIE.

GUSA (STAB) GUSA

I'M SURE THEY'D SUSPECT IT WAS A FIGHT.

IT'S NOT THE TYPE OF INJURY YOU COULD GET ACCI-DENTALLY.

UGH...

Drop by the bar later. I'll ask Kazami to have a look at you and give you some medicine.

I SEE... THE POLICE ARE KEEPING AN EYE ON YOU TOO, SO THIS ISN'T GOOD.

INJURIES WORRY ME.

No arguing. Just get it treated.

O-OKAY.

GAKU (SLUMP)

LOOK, ALL I NEED IS TO STOP THE BLEEDING...

...CAN COME BACK TO HAUNT YOU LATER.

AN INJURY THAT'S NOT TREATED PROPERLY...

Polka, Polka.

I need you to ask her something, just don't let her know you're getting it from me.

FEAR

......

CLARISSA... SO YOUR VISION REALLY IS AS I FEARED...

138

HOW DID YOU KNOW ABOUT THIS HABAKI PERSON, CLARISSA-SAN?

UM...

Y-YES. THE, UH, POLICE ALSO...

...MENTIONED A PERSON NAMED "HOSOROGI-SAN," SO...

...YOU'RE CURIOUS?

I WAS ONLY PUTTING DOWN ROOTS.

...YOU'RE RIGHT.

IN THE END... THE POLICE GOT TO HIM FIRST.

THAT'S ALL I CAN SAY.

!

IT CAN'T BE...

JUST WHO...?

ZAAAA (FSHHH)

...YOU'RE SURE THIS IS WHAT YOU WANT?

I PLANTED A GPS CHIP IN HIS SLEEVE.

I see.

So you can get Habaki's location.

...YES.

Tozawa-san.

I KNOW THAT MY FATHER... LUIS KURAKI, SAVED YOUR WIFE ONCE.

YES. I'VE THOUGHT IT THROUGH, AND I'M SURE.

DO YOU FEEL SO INDEBTED TO ME THAT YOU WOULD BETRAY YOUR OWN SUPERVISOR, TSUBAKI IWANOME?

IT'S NOT ABOUT REPAYING ANY DEBT.

THIS IS MY *PERSONAL* DECISION.

I DON'T KNOW WHAT IT IS, BUT...

I DON'T THINK THIS INCIDENT FALLS INTO THE CATEGORY OF EVEN A TROUBLEMAKER.

MY, MY.

...You're awfully over-protective of him.

I DON'T WANT HIM TO STRAY FROM THAT PATH LIKE I DID.

I WANT CHIEF IWANOME TO BE AN UPSTANDING POLICE INSPECTOR.

UNTIL HE'S...

HE'S VERY STRONG, BUT HE'S STILL FRAGILE.

...I WANT THEM TO WALK THE STRAIGHT AND NARROW.

NO...UNTIL COMPS-3 HAS MATURED...

THAT'S ALL THIS IS ABOUT.

OKAY! LET'S START BY TAKING A FRESH LOOK AT SENIOR COMMISSIONER HABAKI'S CALL LOG.

ARASE AND I WILL HUNT DOWN WHAT INFORMATION WE CAN TOO.

*he pas...
...hooses
...iors are
...trusts ...
...h the west s...
...ace indicated, there's
...one more garage.
There's a signpost.
The key is behind
the first 383 mirror.*

SEE WHO'S HAD ANY CONTACT WITH HABAKI AND THE POLICE OFFICER WHO KILLED HIMSELF.

NOT ONLY THAT. CHECK ALL SURVEILLANCE CAMERAS BOTH INSIDE THE PRECINCT AND AROUND TOWN.

...I KNOW IT'S NOT FAIR TO YOU, BUT...

...I MIGHT STILL BE A LITTLE EMOTIONAL, YOU KNOW?

YOU SURE ARE PULLING OUT ALL THE STOPS.

SO WE'LL JUST NEED HIM TO COME TO US.

I'VE REALIZED THAT EVEN IF I CHASE AFTER HOSOROGI, I'LL NEVER CATCH UP TO HIM.

I HEARD THAT HE SOMEHOW GOT IN TOUCH EARLIER, BUT......

HAVE HIM COME TO US? HOW...?

WE'RE GOING TO COMPLETELY SMOKE OUT THE ORGANIZATION THAT SENIOR COMMISSIONER HABAKI IS A PART OF.

WE'LL USE FORCE.

WE'RE GOING TO ARREST EVERY BASTARD WHO WAS CONTROLLING THEM.

Under the protection of Sabara-mond—

FIRE-BREATH-ING... BUG...

FIRE...

IT CAN'T BE...

I see, lie low for the time being.

IT'S LIKELY "SABARAMOND" IS THE KEY WORD HERE.

HE SAID IT.

Don't worry. I'll shield your location from the Shinoyama family.

SABARA-MOND.

I HEARD HIM SAY IT.

BASTARD CHILD.

145

......

I'M JUST MAKING A PLACE THAT HOSOROGI-SAN WILL COME HOME TO.

UM...

P...... Polka!?

I'M SORRY FOR DOING THIS WITHOUT YOUR PERMISSION, BUT......

LET'S SAY, UH...I WERE TO FIND HOSOROGI-SAN'S SOUL...

IS THERE ANYTHING YOU'D WANT TO TELL HIM?

?

HE—MIYABI-SAN WOULDN'T LIKE TO SEE WHAT I'VE TURNED INTO.

...I TRAMPLED ALL OVER HIS WISHES.

AFTER HE DIED...

AS MY GRANDFATHER SAYS, I AM SOMEONE WHO'S TAKEN THE MEDIATORS TO THE DARK SIDE.

THAT'S AN UNDENIABLE TRUTH, AND I HAVE NO REGRETS ABOUT IT.

BUT I AM WHO I AM.

ANYWAY, THERE'S A LOT I WANT TO TELL HIM.

BUT THERE'S ONE THING I SHOULD SAY TO HIM FIRST.

SO...

...IF I COULD TELL HIM SOMETHING, THERE'S JUST ONE THING I'D WANT TO SAY.

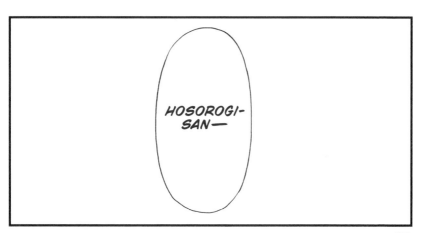

HOSOROGI-SAN—

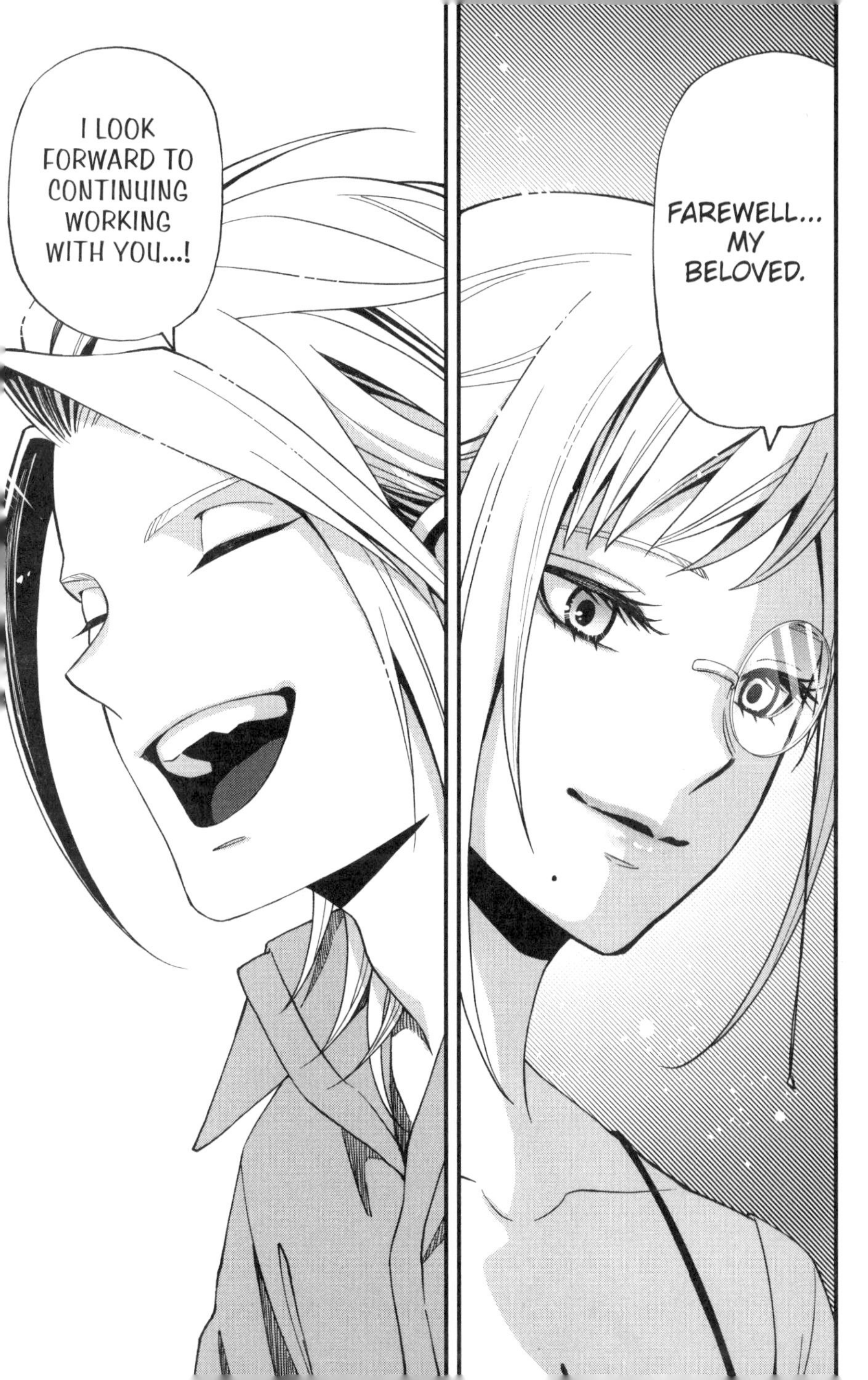
FAREWELL... MY BELOVED.
I LOOK FORWARD TO CONTINUING WORKING WITH YOU...!

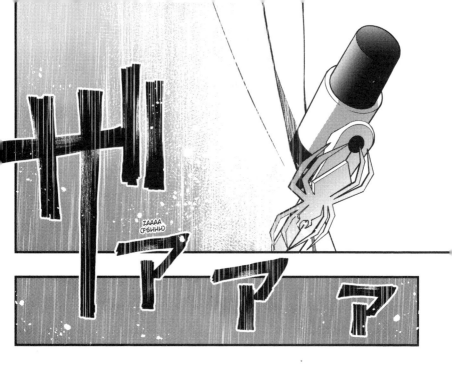

ZAAAA
(FSHHH)

...UHH.

PACHI
(BLINK)
ぱち

WHAT
...?

UMBRELLA: WATCH OUT FOR FIRES

KA
GYAKO

KUH
KUH
KUH.

...WHO'S
THIS?

...UHH.

MISAKI-CHAN! TAKUMI-KUN!

CLOSED

KEE-HEE-HEE! GLAD YOU COULD MAKE IT!

......!

MISAKI-CHAN... YOU SEEM JUST FINE.

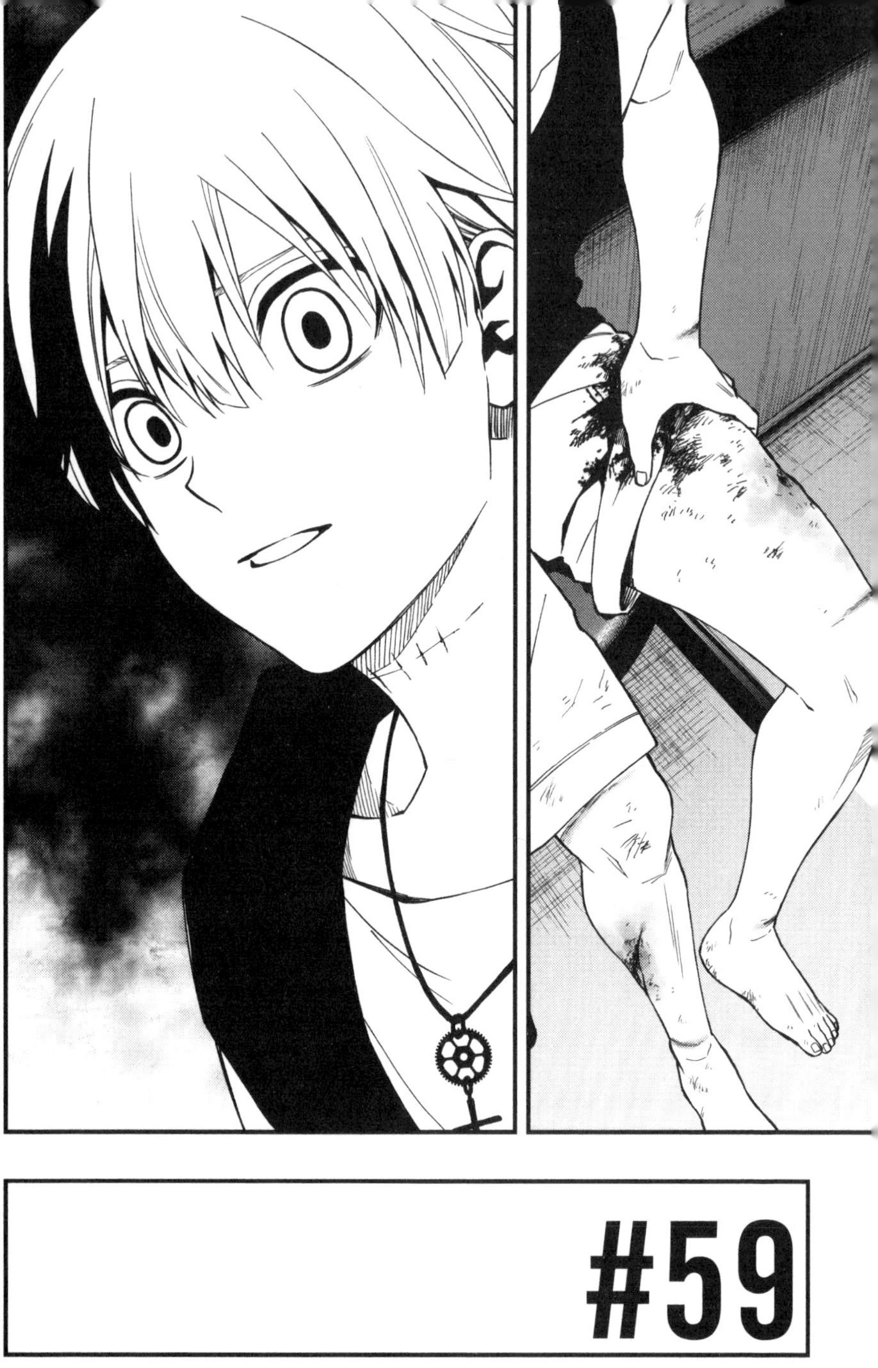

#59

HUH? YOU CAN DO THAT?

IF YOU LIKE, I COULD USE A FLESH-RESTORING SPELL...

MOWOW OW!

TA-KUMI-KUN.

...NO THANKS, I'LL STICK WITH THE REGULAR TREATMENT.

I CAN HEAL ANYTHING THAT'S DEAD, SO I'D HAVE TO MAKE PART OF YOUR BODY A ZOMBIE FIRST...

...OKAY.

IF I'M EVER MORTALLY WOUNDED, THOUGH, YOU CAN BET I'LL BE ASKING YOU THEN.

IF I WANT A WORLD WHERE I CAN LIVE IN PEACE WITH EVERYONE...

IT ISN'T ENOUGH FOR ME TO DO THINGS HALFWAY.

THINGS CAN'T CARRY ON LIKE THIS.

...I NEED TO BE WILLING TO TAKE MORE DETERMINED STEPS TOWARD THAT END.

...I HAVE TO GO MUCH DEEPER...

AS THE "CORPSE GOD"...

...INTO THIS WORLD...

HMM.

......

A MOMENT OF YOUR TIME.

FIRE-BREATHING BUG-KUN?

THAT COULD BE AMUSING, DEPENDING ON WHO HE IS...

IDEALLY AN ALIEN OR SOMEONE WITH SUPER-NATURAL POWERS...

I CAME HERE, BRIMMING WITH EXCITEMENT AT BEING SUMMONED BY YOU FOR THE FIRST TIME EVER, BUT...... YOU AREN'T JUST TRYING TO GET ME ARRESTED FOR KIDNAPPING, ARE YOU?

EVEN A YOKAI WOULD DO! FOR EXAMPLE, IF YOU KIDNAPPED SOMEONE YOU BELIEVED TO BE RICH, BUT THEY TURNED OUT TO BE THE EARLESS PIG YOUKAI FROM AMAMI OSHIMA: THE MINKIRAUWA!

CHANCES ARE I'D BE KILLED, BUT THAT WOULD JUST BE A MINOR DETAIL IN THE FACE OF A SUPERNATURAL PHENOMENON!

IF THE PERSON I KIDNAPPED WAS ACTUALLY A SUPERIOR BEING WHO POSSESSED TRULY TERRIFYING POWERS...

THE MINKIRAUWA WOULD PASS THROUGH THE LEGS OF ALL THE KIDNAPPERS AND TAKE THEIR LIVES!

MINKIRAUWA: ANY HUMAN WHOSE LEGS IT WALKS BETWEEN WILL DIE.

...THEN WE'D BE IN BUSINESS!

THEN I'D USE MAGIC TO CUT OFF THE LOWER HALF OF MY BODY, ALLOWING ME TO DEAL WITH HIM USING JUST MY UPPER HALF!

VS

SINCE "LOWER HALF OF THE BODY"-KUN DOESN'T KNOW HOW TO OPERATE ON ITS OWN, I WOULD LIKE IT TO RETURN TO THE SOIL, BECOME A FOREST, AND CONTINUOUSLY SEND NUTRIENTS WIRELESSLY TO "UPPER HALF OF THE BODY"-KUN.

SUPERHUMAN PHOTOSYNTHESIS

YEAH... THIS IS THE WISDOM OF A MAGICIAN! THE MIRACLE OF THE ILLUSIONIST!

NOT GOOD. I DON'T HAVE A CLUE WHAT HE'S TALKING ABOUT.

JUDGING BY HIS LINE OF THINKING, HE'S ON A A TOTALLY DIFFERENT PLANE THAN ME...THAT MUCH I'VE FIGURED OUT, BUT...

THAT'S ENOUGH JOKING FOR NOW.

NOW, THEN.

...I'D ONLY GET SWALLOWED WHOLE IF I TRIED TO UNDERSTAND HIM. HE'S A CONNECTION I DON'T WANT TO ASSOCIATE WITH.

AN INNOCENT, AVERAGE CITIZEN WHO HAPPENED TO LEARN FIRE-BREATHING BUG-KUN'S TRUE IDENTITY... OR NOT?

WHO IS THIS WE HAVE SITTING HERE?

...YOU'RE FRIENDS WITH HABAKI FROM THE PRECINCT... OR SOMETHING LIKE THAT?

PER-HAPS...

UMBRELLA: WATCH OUT FOR FIRES

FIRE-BREATHING BUG-KUN, SO FAR YOU'VE BURNED EVERY LAST PERSON RELATED TO THE ORGANIZATION...

...BUT YOU MUST HAVE REALIZED YOUR WAY OF DOING THINGS HAD DRAWBACKS, RIGHT?

IN OTHER WORDS, HE'S A PARTY CONCERNED WITH THIS SYMBOL.

!

PAN (CLAP)

SO YOU TRIED A NEW APPROACH!

WHEN THE ORGANIZATION GOES PUBLIC...

...THE SITUATION WILL CHANGE DRASTICALLY.

THE ROOT OF THE ORGANIZATION IS KEY. REACHING THAT ROOT, WHICH MUST BE STAMPED OUT...

IN OTHER WORDS! HAVING DRAGGED THIS MAN AND HABAKI TO THE FOREFRONT, YOU MEAN TO RELY ON MY ABILITIES... RIGHT?

THAT'S EXACTLY...

...IT.

......

SOMETIMES BEING A MAGICIAN REQUIRES THE ART OF CONVERSATION... THIS MUCH IS ONLY NATURAL FOR ME.

... MOTH.

AS I'D EXPECT...

...FROM YOU...

THIS SAVES US TIME.

I THOUGHT HE WAS JUST A CRIMINAL WITH A SCREW LOOSE, BUT...

......!!

...FROM WHAT I'M HEARING NOW... EVEN THOUGH THAT DIRIGIBLE INCIDENT LOOKED UNPLANNED, THIS WAS ACTUALLY ALL THOROUGHLY CALCULATED.

THOUGH I'D HOPED TO REACT WITH A "D'OOOOH!" AFTER BEING TOLD, "YOU'RE TOTALLY WRONG!"......

D'OOOOH!

I ONLY MEANT IT AS A JOKE, BUT TO THINK I'VE ACTUALLY HIT THE NAIL ON THE HEAD......

TEARS OF SADNESS MAY SERVE TO MOISTEN ONE'S THROAT WHEN IT'S DRY AND YOU WANT TO SCREAM YOUR WISHES......

"SADNESS"?

?

WELL THEN, THAT'S ALL SETTLED.

KUH...

I WISH I'D BEEN RIGHT ABOUT IT BEING A YOKAI OR ALIEN INSTEAD...!

...THAT YOU'RE INVOLVED WITH ALL THE TROUBLE-MAKERS.

ぽん

PON (PAT)

ALSO...... I CAN TELL...

UM...I HAVE NO IDEA WHAT ANY OF THIS HAS TO DO WITH ME, SO COULD YOU JUST LET ME GO HOME?

YOU'VE GOT THE SMELL OF SOMEONE WHO'S KILLED COUNTLESS PEOPLE.

DO YOU HAVE ANY PROOF? BEYOND YOUR NOSE, I MEAN.

SO ANYTHING I DO WILL BE FORGIVEN, OR I'M SCREWED!

......

WORRY NOT. MY PRIDE IS STILL IN A JAIL CELL.

HEH HEH HEH.

BI (JAB)

PRIDE

IF I'M JUST AN ORDINARY CITIZEN, WON'T THIS WHOLE MIX-UP BE A TERRIBLE BLOW TO YOUR PRIDE?

THE FACT OF THE MATTER IS, I AM A BOTHER TO ORDINARY CITIZENS! MY APOLOGIES!

IF YOU'RE AWARE OF THAT, THEN WOULD YOU STOP IT WITH ALL THIS!?

I DON'T QUITE FOLLOW.

164

AS A RESULT OF MY ACTIONS, A LOT OF COMPANIES' STOCK PRICES TOOK A NOSEDIVE.

IT WAS A PARTICULAR NUISANCE WHEN I ABDUCTED PRIME MINISTER KUBIKI-GAWARA.

KEEP AN EYE ON OUR STOCKS, AND INTERVENE IF NEED BE.

IF THE MEDIA CATCHES WIND OF THIS, AS A SECURITY COMPANY, WE MIGHT NEED TO GET "INVOLVED" AGAIN...

TON (THMP)

IT SEEMS SOLITAIRE INFILTRATED THE POLICE STATION.

LOOKS LIKE THERE WAS MOVEMENT IN POLKA'S BUILDING TOO.

SHEESH. IT'S A REAL HEADACHE TRYING TO READ THE MOVEMENTS OF CRIMINALS WHO CAUSE MAYHEM JUST FOR THE FUN OF IT.

...YOUR SISTER'S BODYGUARD AND THE GIRL WE USUALLY SEE AT THE BUILDING CAME BACK, BUT...

YES... AFTER LISA KURAKI AND POLKA SHINOYAMA LEFT...

AND YOUR SISTER'S BODYGUARD HAD ONE OF HIS PROSTHETIC LIMBS CUT OFF.

IT'S POSSIBLE THEY HAD A RUN-IN WITH AN ENEMY FORCE OF SOME KIND.

...THE INFORMANT WAS WOUNDED.

SO FORMAL. EVEN IF HE'S A BODYGUARD IN MY GRANDFATHER'S EMPLOY, HE'S STILL PART OR YOUR FAMILY, REMEMBER?

HE CUT TIES WITH THE LEI FAMILY A LONG TIME AGO. YOU NEEDN'T CONCERN YOURSELF WITH HIM, TAKERU-SAMA.

...BUT EVEN SO, HE IS STILL *RATHER* CAPABLE.

HWA-CHOO!

OUR OPPONENT ISN'T JUST SOME SMALL-TIME PUNK...... IS WHAT YOU'RE SAYING.

TON (TAP)

トン トン

TON

OH?

UNFORTU-NATELY, THEY MAY ALREADY BE REACHING THEIR HAND TOWARD US.

...IT COULD BE THEY HAVE ALREADY MADE A PREEMPTIVE ATTACK.

WE NEED TO FIGURE OUT JUST HOW FAR THIS ENEMY'S HAND REACHES.

SINCE NIGHTFALL, A NUMBER OF THE LOOKOUTS SURROUNDING THE BUILDING HAVE BEEN ATTACKED.

THEY WERE KNOCKED OUT FROM BEHIND AND THEIR CELL PHONES WERE TAKEN.

HM......? SO THEY'RE ATTACKING INDIVIDUALS AS WELL?

WHAT'S MORE... ALL THE MONEY IN MY BANK ACCOUNT HAS DISAPPEARED.

...IN OTHER WORDS... SOMEONE IS LOOKING FOR INFORMATION.

ROGER.

LOOK INTO IT, BAO.

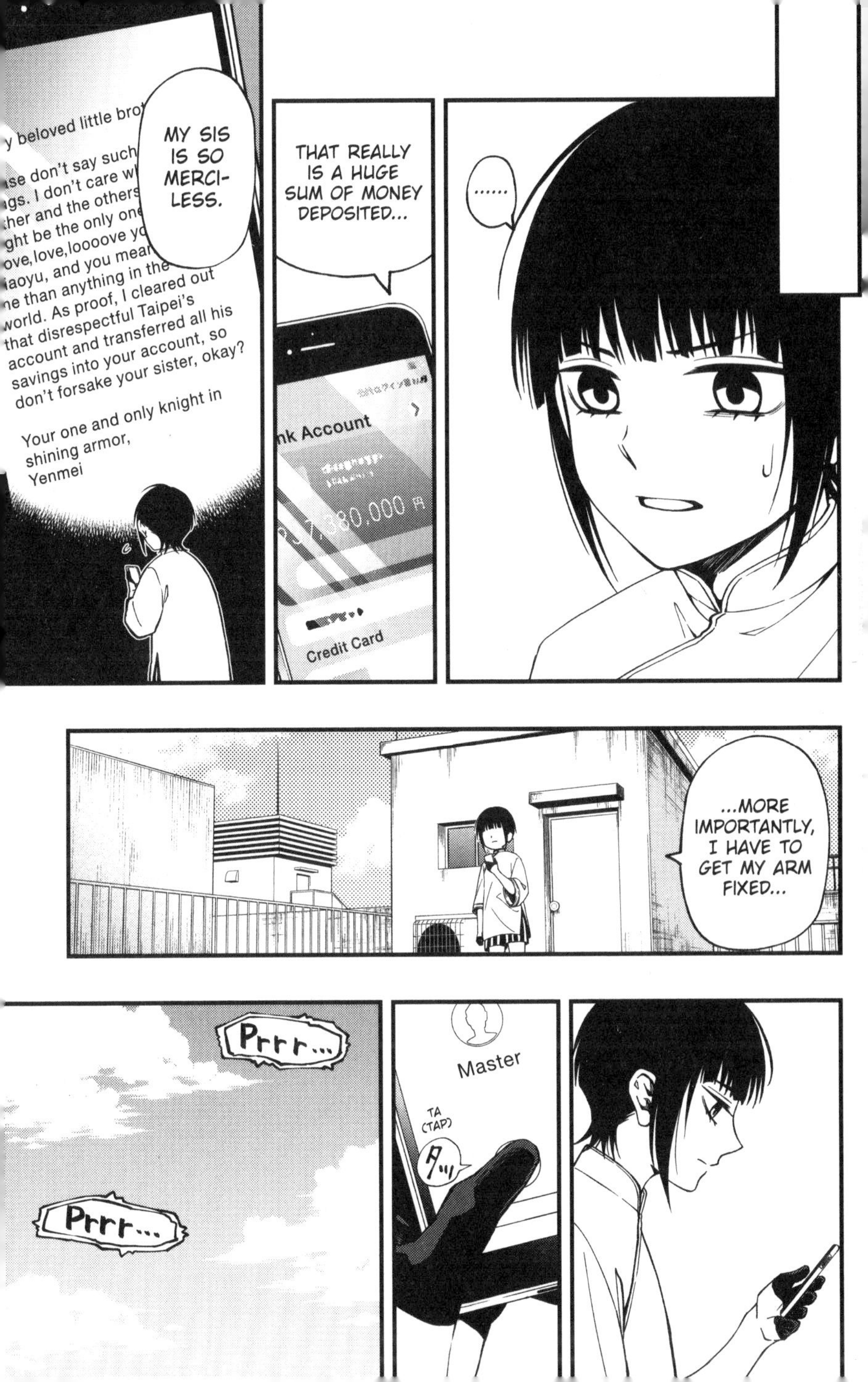
......
THAT REALLY IS A HUGE SUM OF MONEY DEPOSITED...
nk Account
380,000 円
Credit Card
MY SIS IS SO MERCI-LESS.
y beloved little brot
se don't say such
gs. I don't care wh
her and the others
ght be the only one
ove,love,loooove yo
aoyu, and you mean
ne than anything in the
world. As proof, I cleared out
that disrespectful Taipei's
account and transferred all his
savings into your account, so
don't forsake your sister, okay?
Your one and only knight in
shining armor,
Yenmei
...MORE IMPORTANTLY, I HAVE TO GET MY ARM FIXED...
Master
TA (TAP)
Prrr...
Prrr...

I heard. One of your arms got ruined.

!

M-MASTER... UM...

It's me.

Hey.

......YES. I HAD A RUN-IN WITH THE AGAKURA.

HE MUST'VE HEARD FROM THE TEAM WATCHING OVER THE BUILDING...

And I hear you protected the guys from the building too.

What matters is that you're alive.

HUH!? SO THE SURVEILLANCE GROUP FOUND OUT ABOUT AGAKURA TOO?

Ah, yeah, I heard about that too.

U... UM.

......!

Xiao-yu.

You did well... Thanks.

UH... MY KNEE WILL MAKE IT, BUT MY ARM'S COMPLETELY DESTROYED...

...SO...IT LOOKS LIKE I'LL HAVE TO GET BY ONE-HANDED FOR A WHILE.

So how are your arms and legs?

ピタ
PITA
(FREEZE)

...Y-YOU DON'T HAVE TO THANK ME, MASTER!

YOU GAVE ME THESE FOUR LIMBS, MASTER, AND I...

I'M SO SORRY.

The *guy behind you* says he'll take care of it for you.

HUH?

OH, AND... YOU MIGHT NOT HAVE TO GO WITH ONLY ONE HAND AT ALL.

DON'T WORRY ABOUT IT.

BEHIND ME...?

...XIAOYU-KUN.

THE FAKE POLKA!

!?

HE COULD HAVE KILLED ME.

I DIDN'T SENSE HIM COMING AT ALL.

WHEN DID HE GET HERE!?

HOW WAS HE ABLE TO BE SO QUIET!?

THIS DOESN'T HAPPEN TO ME!

I SLIPPED UP!

MISAKI-CHAN TOLD ME ABOUT YOU SAVING TAKUMI-KUN.

MY JOB IS TO PROTECT THE SHINOYAMAS.

...I ONLY ACTED BECAUSE NOT DOING SO MAY HAVE ALLOWED HARM TO COME TO MISTRESS SAYO.

......

......MY JOB IS TO PROTECT THE SHINO-YAMAS.

......

...PLEASE LET ME PREPARE YOU A NEW ARM.

...I DON'T TRUST YOU.

THAT'S WHY...

I COULD TELL RIGHT AWAY BECAUSE OF THE UNIQUE COLOR OF THE SOUL ENVELOPING YOUR LIMBS.

THE PEOPLE IN THE CEILING... AND UNDER THE FLOOR-BOARDS TOO. PLEASE.

!?

WELL, WELL, SO YOU NOTICED THEM TOO.

THE PERSON WHO WAS UNDER THE FLOOR IN ROZAN-SAN'S ROOM...WAS YOU, WASN'T IT?

OH, UH...

SORRY ABOUT THAT. SO WHERE WERE WE?

......

174

I'LL EXPLAIN EVERYTHING, INCLUDING THAT.

"COLOR OF THE SOUL"...? WHAT ARE YOU TALKING ABOUT...!?

THAT'S ALSO HOW I KNEW YOU ALREADY RECOGNIZED ME AS A FAKE.

THAT'S WHY...

AND I KNOW THAT YOU CAN'T TRUST ME.

I DOUBT YOU'LL UNDERSTAND.

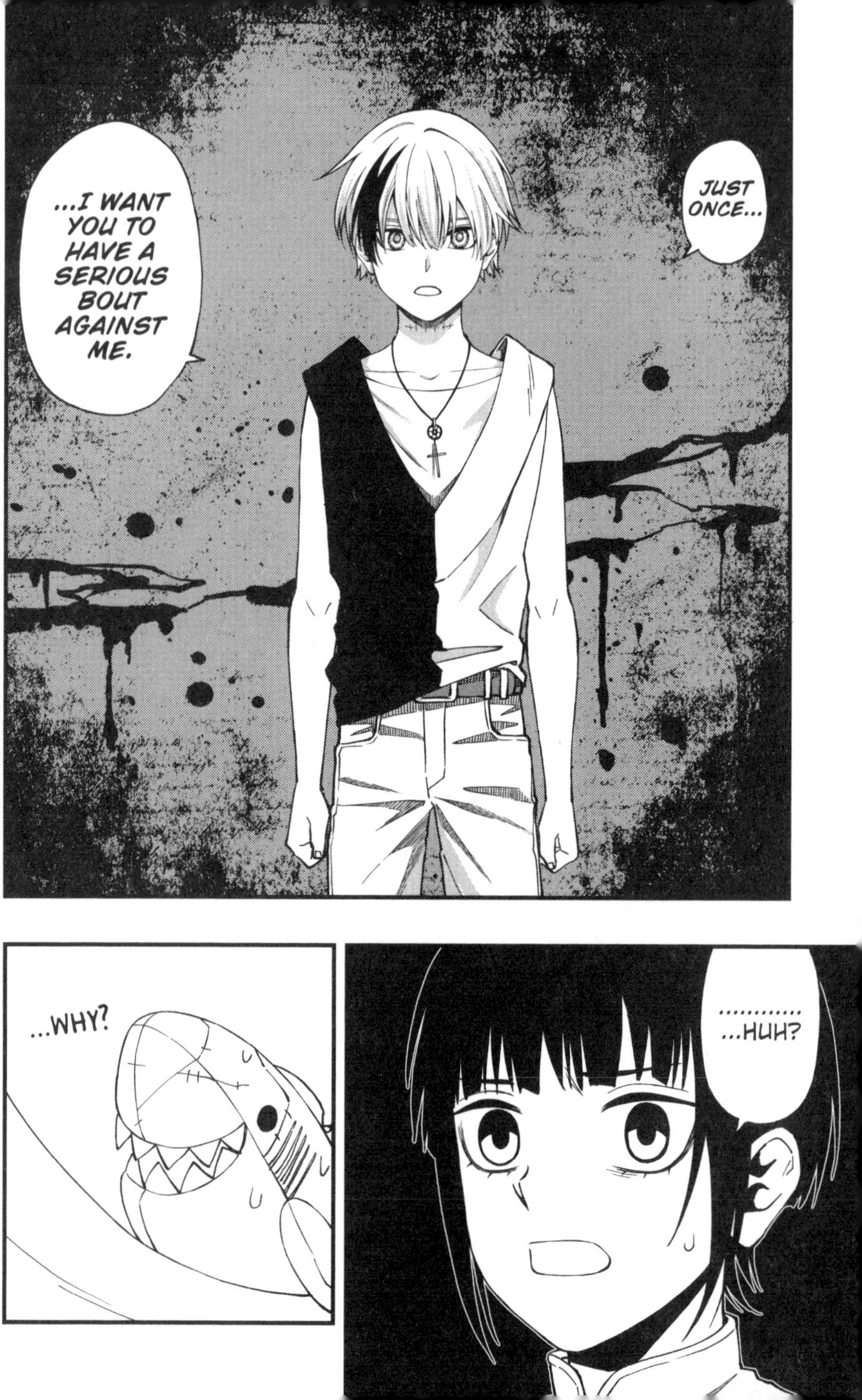
JUST ONCE...
...I WANT YOU TO HAVE A SERIOUS BOUT AGAINST ME.
....HUH?
...WHY?

#60

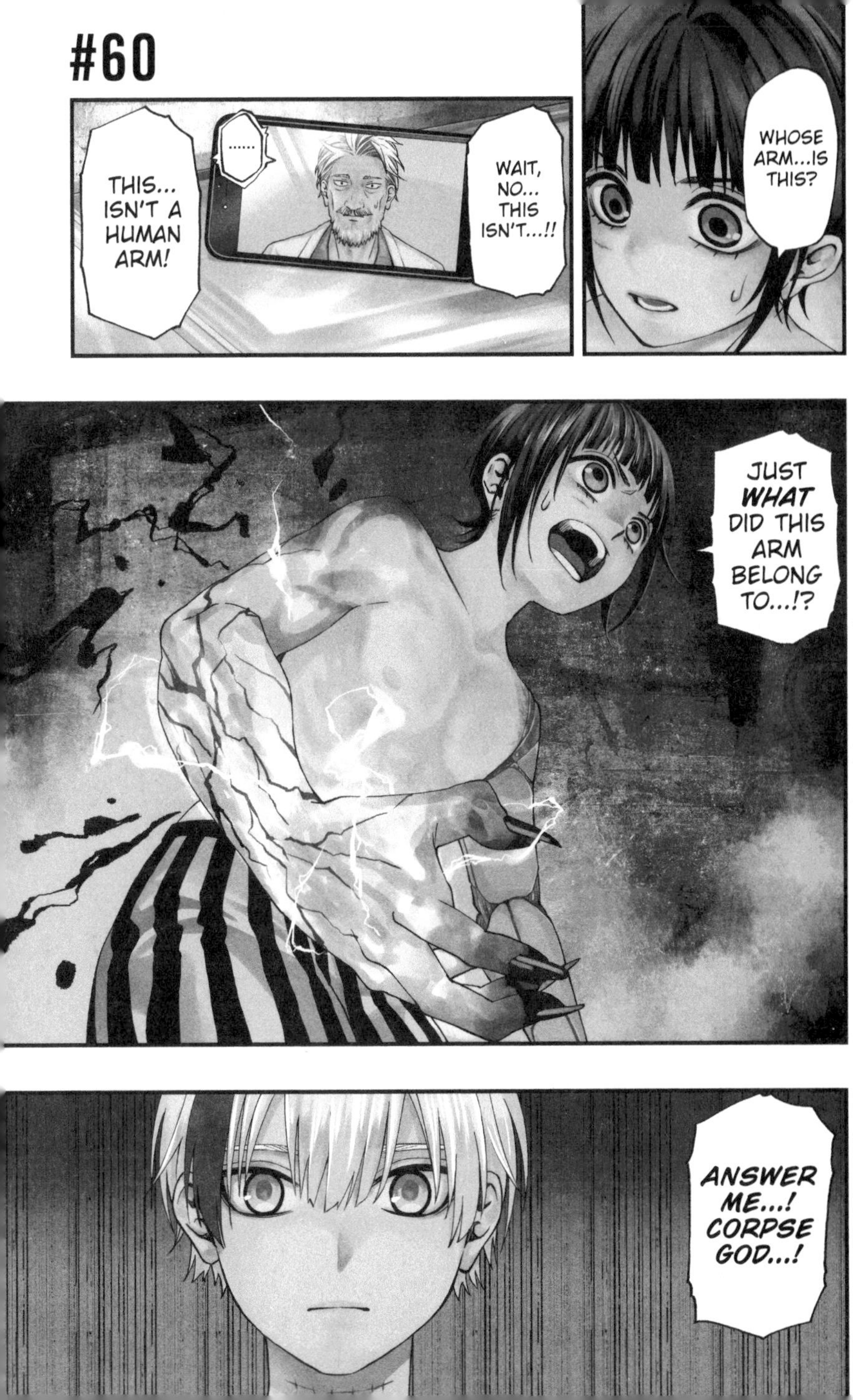
WHOSE ARM...IS THIS?
WAIT, NO... THIS ISN'T...!!
......
THIS... ISN'T A HUMAN ARM!
JUST *WHAT* DID THIS ARM BELONG TO...!?
ANSWER ME...! CORPSE GOD...!

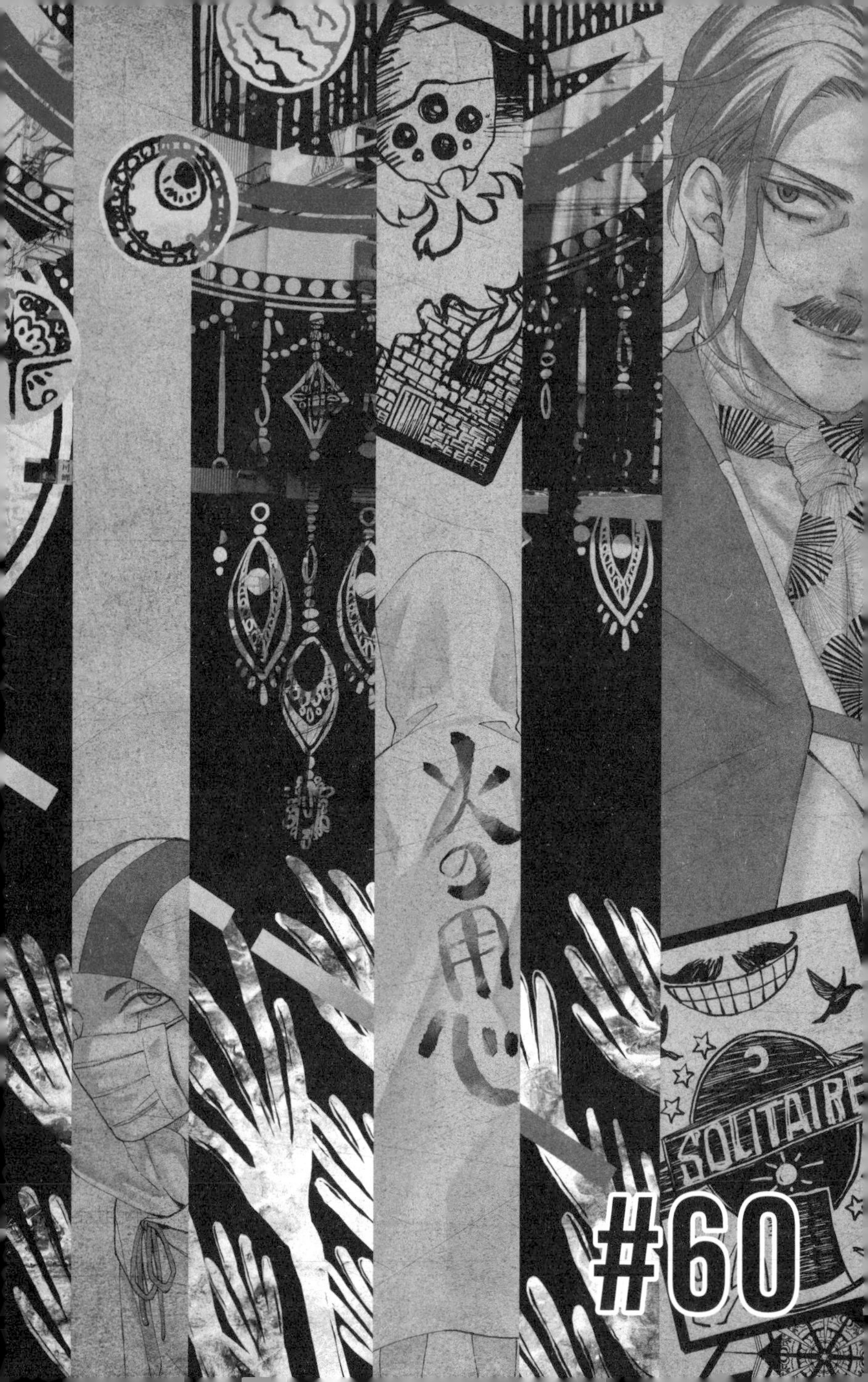
火の用心
SOLITAIRE
#60

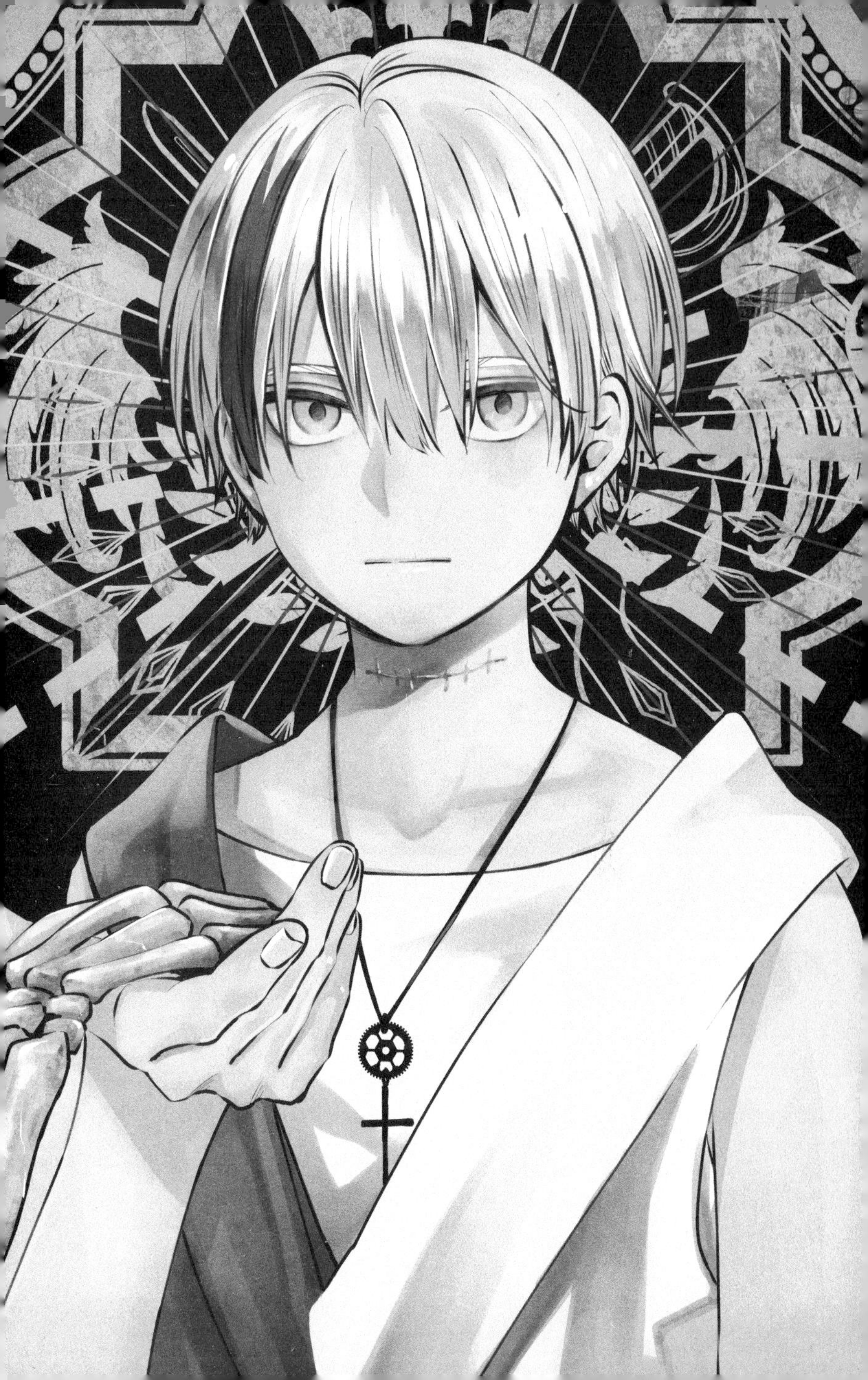

DEAD MOUNT
DEATH PLAY

ONE HOUR AGO...

NO, I'M NOT TRYING TO BE ARROGANT...

I'LL MAKE YOU REGRET YOUR ARRO-GANCE.

YOU FIGURE IF YOU KNOCK ME DOWN WHEN I HAVE ONLY ONE ARM, YOU'LL HAVE AN EDGE ON ME GOING FORWARD?

HMPH...

Ooooh, how I envy the young.

THIS IS JUST WHAT I WANTED. I'M GOING TO EXPOSE WHO YOU REALLY ARE TO THE MASTER.

I DON'T CARE WHY YOU'RE DOING THIS.

...I WILL NOT LET MY GUARD DOWN.

IN OTHER WORDS, I SHOULD BE WARY THAT ANYTHING SAKIMIYA-SAN CAN DO, THE FAKE POLKA CAN PROBABLY DO TOO.

THE STATE OF SAKIMIYA-SAN'S BODY IS PROBABLY ALSO HIS DOING......

I ALREADY KNOW HE'S MORE THAN JUST A FAKE.

...I'M NOT THINKING THAT AT ALL.

YOU SAVED TAKUMI-KUN. THERE'S NO NEED FOR YOU TO DEFER TO ME.

...DON'T THINK I'LL BOW MY HEAD TO YOU IN FRONT OF THE MASTER.

SO...

ZA
(ZSH)

ENOUGH TALK. TAKE YOUR STANCE.

......?

ALTHOUGH... IT IS MY *POWER*, SO IT'S ALMOST THE SAME THING...

...I DIDN'T REALLY MEAN MY BODY.

......I SAID I WANTED YOU TO HAVE A SERIOUS BOUT AGAINST ME, BUT...

183

HUH?

JUST WHAT ARE YOU—

?

THOUGH I CAN'T SUMMON HIM FOR LONG...

YOUR OPPONENT WILL BE THIS DUAL-FANGED TIGER.

ZUN
(THOOM)

SHOW ME YOUR STRENGTH AS BEST YOU CAN.

GRRR
ooo

GO
(WHAMMM)

A HALLUCI-NATION!? HYPNOSIS!?

I CAN'T WRAP MY HEAD AROUND THIS! WHAT IS THIS MONSTER!?

TAN (TMP)

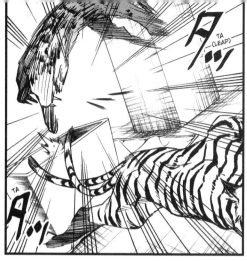

ARE YOU TELLING ME IT'S REAL...?

WHAT I KNOW FOR SURE IS THAT THE FAKE POLKA IS THE ONE WHO CREATED THIS SITUATION.

CRAAH!

WHATEVER... I'LL FIGURE IT OUT LATER.

GRAH!

GRRR...

!

KA
(FLASH)

IIDA
(DASH)

GAKI
(SNAP)

ヒュン
HYUN
(WHIP)

THAT WAS A CLOSE ONE.

EVEN IN THAT BLINDING LIGHT... I CAN SEE THE COLOR OF YOUR SOUL.

....!

...HAS A KEEN SENSE OF SMELL.

AND THE DUAL-FANGED TIGER...

......!!

EVEN IF MY LIMITED MAGIC MEANS THE DUAL-FANGED TIGER'S NOT AS FAST AS THEY COULD BE, HE'S STILL ABLE TO AVOID THEIR ATTACKS WITH JUST ONE ARM.

You're capable of things even more amazing than I'd imagined.

NO... XIAOYU-KUN IS THE AMAZING ONE.

...I must say.

......

THOUGH HE WAS A LITTLE RUSHED.

AND HE MADE THE RIGHT DECISION TO KEEP HIS COOL AND TARGET ME, THE ONE INVOKING IT.

When I got that phone call from you last night, I'll admit, it gave me a chill.

IT'S EASY TO TELL HIM... "DON'T PUSH YOURSELF TOO HARD. IF YOU WANT TO RUN AWAY, YOU CAN RUN AWAY."

I thought he'd do something reckless and put his life in danger.

The Agakura are the ones who picked off his limbs.

IN MY TIME, I'VE SEEN PLENTY OF PEOPLE WHO PRIORITIZE THEIR FEELINGS OVER THEIR LIVES.

...I CAN SEE THAT.

But Xiaoyu's the type who, when someone tells him he can retreat, it makes him all the more determined to do the opposite.

...IN HOLDING BACK, ONE CAN END UP LOSING SO MUCH MORE.

Still, are you okay with this?

If your goal is to live in peace, then I'd have figured you'd want to keep your secret from Xiaoyu.

191

...I'VE DECIDED THAT I'LL DISTANCE MYSELF FROM THAT PEACE FOR A LITTLE WHILE.

FOR THE SAKE OF MY FUTURE PEACE...

RRR!

HE'S COMING AT ME FROM MY PARALYZED SIDE...!

KUH...!

RAWR!

PITA
(PAUSE)

PURR...

THANK
YOU,
GUFA.
RAFA.

MROW...

...OKAY,
I'VE
GOT THE
PICTURE.

AH!
HEY,
NOW!

BERON
(LICK)

BIKU
(FLINCH)

WHA
...?

HAAH...

...I ADMIT DEFEAT.

HUH?

SORRY. IT SEEMS THEY LIKE YOU...

? BERO BERO (LICK) BERO BERO BERO ! BERO

!?

UH? WELL, OKAY, THEN.

1 FUN (SNUFF) FUN PERO PERO PERO PERO (LICK) PERO

DO AS YOU LIKE.

I CAN SEE THE EXTENT OF YOUR POWER NOW.

......

BERO BERO

IN ANY CASE, I THINK IT'D BE BEST IF YOU TOOK A SHOWER.

ザァァ...
ZAAAA
(FSHHH)

...NO, THAT'S JUST AN EXCUSE.

I TOOK THAT BOUT AS SERIOUSLY AS ANY I'VE FOUGHT.

IF ONLY MY RIGHT ARM AND LEGS WERE IN FULL WORKING ORDER...

ザァ
ァ
ZAAA

BUT HE...

...WITH THAT INCOMPREHENSIBLE POWER...

195

I'M CERTAIN HE WAS FAR FROM TAKING OUR BOUT SERIOUSLY...

WHAT'S GOING ON...!?

WHAT THE...!

THANK YOU.

DOSUN (PLOP)

CYBORG! MECHA!

HAPPY SHARK DANCE

SO...CAN YOU DO SOMETHING ABOUT MY ARM?

...THIS IS WHAT THE JOINTS LOOK LIKE.

OH. WELCOME BACK.

196

HUH?

...YOUR NAME?

......

SO IT DOESN'T FEEL RIGHT FOR ME TO KEEP REFERRING TO YOU AS "THE FAKE."

...YOUR STRENGTH IS INDISPUTABLE. YOU'RE THE REAL DEAL.

IF YOU'RE NOT POLKA, THEN YOU MUST HAVE A REAL NAME.

...MOST PEOPLE CALL ME...

...THAT'S QUITE THE HEFTY TITLE.

..."CORPSE GOD."

BUT THERE'S NO QUESTION IT'S FITTING FOR A SUPERNATURAL BEING OR APPARITION LIKE YOU.

YEAH, I THINK SO TOO.

I'LL ACCEPT ANY NUMBER OF ROLES.

A PUP-PET.

A SACRI-FICE.

LISTEN... I DON'T CARE WHAT HAPPENS TO ME.

198

ALL I ASK IS THAT YOU NOT TURN THOSE FANGS UPON THE MASTER.

SO... PLEASE.

HUH!?

THAT WAS NEVER MY INTENTION, SO...?

?

I'VE BEEN REALLY GRATEFUL FOR THE WORRY-FREE HUMAN RELATIONS I'VE ENJOYED SO FAR...

NO...IT WASN'T A FIGHT. IT WAS A BOUT... RIGHT?

I WANTED TO SEE HOW YOU FIGHT WITH AS MUCH DETAIL AS POSSIBLE...

HUH?

HUH?

DIDN'T YOU CHALLENGE ME TO THAT FIGHT TO MAKE THE PECKING ORDER CLEAR ONCE AND FOR ALL?

ZUUUN
(GLOOOM)

...BUT FOR YOU, IT WASN'T EVEN A STRUGGLE...

I PUT MY LIFE AND PRIDE ON THE LINE BACK THERE...

WHA...?

HUH!?

I AGREE.

Uhhh...Xiaoyu can be pretty quick to jump to conclusions, but I do blame you on this one, Corpse God.

FORGET IT.

I'M... REALLY SORRY.

SO? WHAT KIND OF TUNE-UP ARE YOU PLANNING TO DO?

I-IN THE EMPIRE, ASSESSING A FIGHTER'S STYLE AND ABILITIES WAS THE BASIC FIRST STEP BEFORE TUNING THEIR WEAPONS...

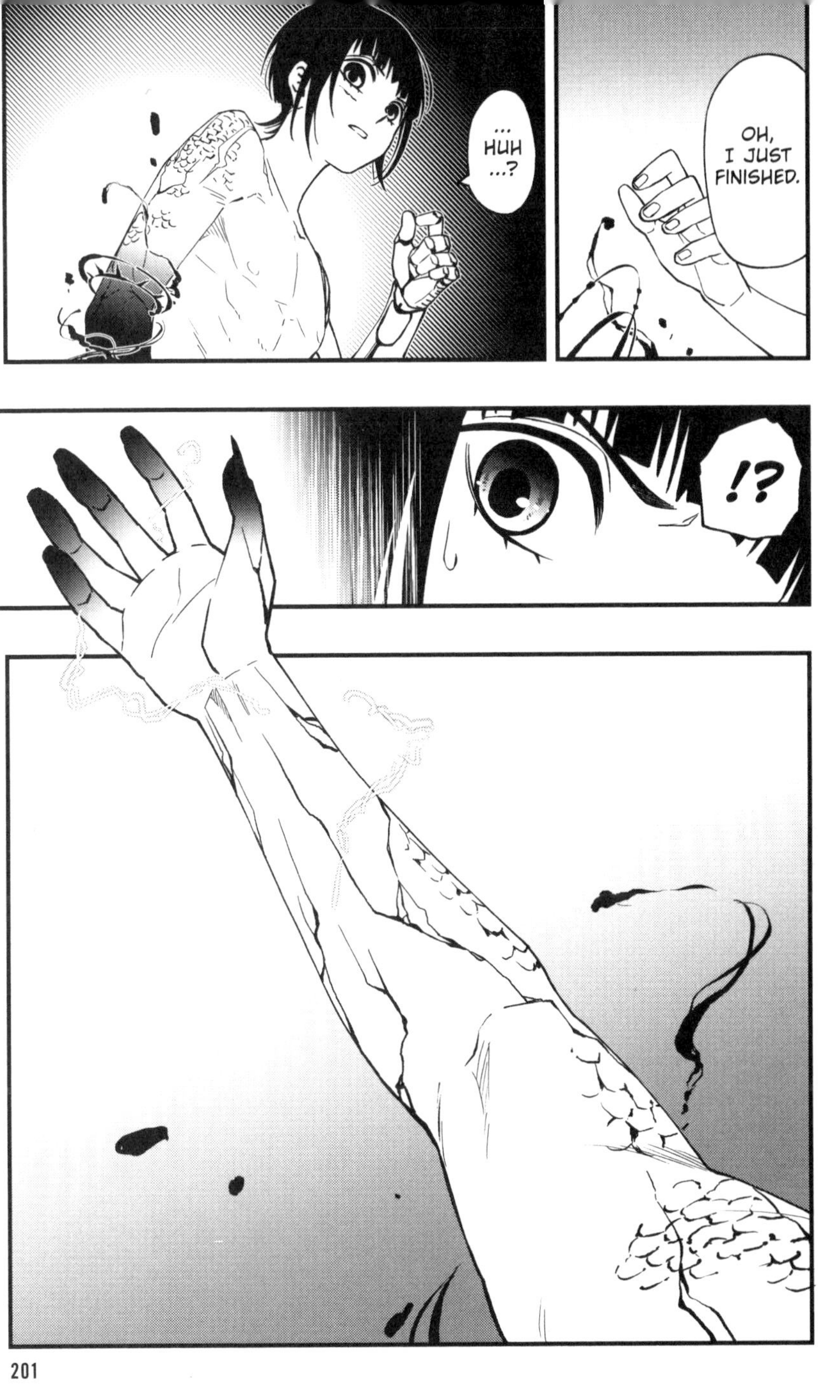
OH, I JUST FINISHED.
... HUH ...?
!?

JUST **WHAT** DID THIS ARM BELONG TO...!?

WAIT, NO... NO, THIS ISN'T!!

THIS... ISN'T A HUMAN ARM!

WHOSE ARM...IS THIS?

ANSWER ME......! CORPSE GOD...!

IT'S THE RIGHT ARM OF THE COLOSSAL LIGHTING DRAGON THAT USED TO BATHE THE WORLD IN ELECTRICITY.

...URD-WIGIA.

...DRA-GON?

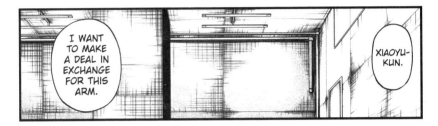

I WANT TO MAKE A DEAL IN EXCHANGE FOR THIS ARM.

XIAOYU-KUN.

AS THE FOURTH-HIGHEST RANKING SORCERER IN THE IMPERIAL COURT...

...I WANT YOU TO MAKE AN ALLIANCE WITH ME.

I'VE GOT JUST THE THING TO SOLVE ALL YOUR PROBLEMS.

I'M TALKING, LIKE, BAGGY PANTS.

IF POSSIBLE, I'D APPRECIATE SOMETHING I CAN WEAR LIKE THIS.

SORRY. BUT SINCE I CAN'T GO HOME, COULD YOU GO BUY ME A CHANGE OF CLOTHES?

THE SHARK PAJAMAS SAYO WAS WEARING IN CHAPTER 25

A SHARK!

JUST REGULAR SWEATS AND A T-SHIRT WILL DO.

SHEESH... THIS IS AN AWFULLY BAD BARGAIN YOU'VE FORCED ME INTO.

DRAGONS REALLY ARE A DIFFERENT BREED.

THE CONDITION FOR FORMING A TWO-HUNDRED-YEAR CONTRACT WITH ME IS THAT I HAVE TO BUY BACK YOUR REMAINS FROM THE GUILD?

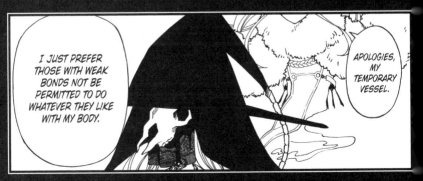

I JUST PREFER THOSE WITH WEAK BONDS NOT BE PERMITTED TO DO WHATEVER THEY LIKE WITH MY BODY.

APOLOGIES, MY TEMPORARY VESSEL.

ON THE OTHER HAND, THE BELOVED PUPIL OF WANDERING BALCONY—THE ONE **WHO KILLED ME**—IS A BOND THAT WILL MORE THAN SUFFICE.

JUST TAKE THIS AS A LESSON THAT THERE ARE THOSE LIKE HIM IN THE WORLD TOO.

DON'T MIND HIM, MY FOOLISH PUPIL.

?

??

KILLED...

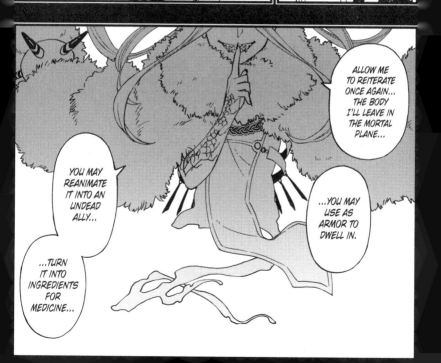

ALLOW ME TO REITERATE ONCE AGAIN... THE BODY I'LL LEAVE IN THE MORTAL PLANE...

YOU MAY REANIMATE IT INTO AN UNDEAD ALLY...

...YOU MAY USE AS ARMOR TO DWELL IN.

...TURN IT INTO INGREDIENTS FOR MEDICINE...

...OR EVEN USE IT TO FORM A NEW BOND WITH SOME- ONE...

#61

SFX: GYURURURURU (SPIN)

C'MON...DON'T GO SAYING THINGS THAT'LL PISS OFF THE FANBASE OF EITHER OF THOSE.

I THINK NOVELS THAT HAVE ADVENTURERS GUILDS HAVE A LOT IN COMMON WITH SHARK MOVIES.

EVEN THOUGH THEY ALL FUNCTION SIMILARLY, THE AUTHORS ADD SOME ORIGINAL ELEMENT SO THAT EVERY STORY IS ULTIMATELY ORIGINAL AND UNIQUE, YOU KNOW?

OF COURSE, THERE ARE SOME STORIES WITHOUT A GUILD AT ALL.

I MEAN THE TYPICAL ADVENTURERS GUILD THAT YOU SEE IN STORIES ABOUT BEING REBORN INTO OR MATERIALIZING IN A FANTASY WORLD...

SHARK MOVIES ARE THE SAME. THEY ALL SHARE THE SAME GIMMICK—THE MAN-EATING SHARK— BUT THAT'S WHERE THEY'LL ADD A UNIQUE TWIST. MAYBE THERE'S A TORNADO, OR GHOSTS, OR DEMONS, OR ZOMBIES, OR SHARKS THAT CAN SWIM ON SAND OR THROUGH SNOW. MAYBE IT'S AN ATOMIC SHARK, OR A ROBOT, OR A MECHA, OR JURASSIC, OR THREE-HEADED...(CONDENSED)... OR EVEN SIX-HEADED. AND ALL THESE DIFFERENT ELEMENTS MAKE EACH AND EVERY ONE OF THEM ORIGINAL, SEE?

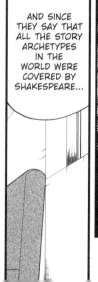

AND SINCE THEY SAY THAT ALL THE STORY ARCHETYPES IN THE WORLD WERE COVERED BY SHAKESPEARE...

YEAH... THAT'S WHY YOU COULD CALL A PERIOD PIECE A SHARK MOVIE... SAME WITH WESTERNS TOO.

YEAH, BUT... AREN'T PERIOD PIECES AND WESTERNS THE SAME WAY?

RIGHT. SO CAN YOU GET TO YOUR POINT?

SHARKSPEARE

...MAYBE SHAKESPEARE WAS A SHARK...?

REPRESENTATIVE WORK: THE TAMING OF THE SHARK

HUH!? ME!?

I'M JUST TRYING TO SAY... WE SHOULD SEE WHAT'S UNIQUE ABOUT THE KIND OF "VAMPIRE" MISAKI-CHAN IS.

IT WOULD ALSO BE TO PREVENT ANY BAD GUYS FROM FINDING OUT HER STRENGTHS OR WEAKNESSES.

I THINK IT'S IMPORTANT FOR US ALL TO KNOW HOW FAR FROM THE USUAL "VAMPIRE" STEREOTYPES MISAKI-CHAN DEVIATES.

DID YOU HAVE TO INCLUDE THE BIT ABOUT SHARK MOVIES?

TALK ABOUT BEATING AROUND THE BUSH...

YEP! ONLY, IT SEEMS A LITTLE BRIGHTER TO ME THAN BEFORE, I GUESS.

BUT I THINK IT'S MUCH EASIER FOR ME TO TURN INTO BATS AT NIGHTTIME.

HOW ABOUT THIS? ARE YOU OKAY WITH SUNLIGHT?

...WELL, YOU'VE GOT A POINT THERE.

AND ANOTHER THING...DO YOU DRINK BLOOD OR ANYTHING?

HM?

YEAH, WELL, THE WHOLE WEAKNESS TO SUNLIGHT THING DEPENDS ON THE STORY.

I WAS CURIOUS ABOUT THAT TOO, SO I ASKED CORPSE GOD A BUNCH OF QUESTIONS.

BUT APPARENTLY VAMPIRES FROM WHERE HE'S FROM ONLY DRINK BLOOD WHEN THEY NEED, LIKE, A PICK-ME-UP.

IN MANGA AND MOVIES, WHEN SOMEBODY GETS BITTEN, THEY EVENTUALLY GET TURNED INTO A VAMPIRE OR GHOUL THEMSELVES...

210

UH-HUH... OKAY, SO BASICALLY IT'S NOT SOMETHING THEY CAN DRINK AS REGULARLY AS WATER OR ALCOHOL.

THOUGH THERE WERE SOME RITUALISTIC TIMES THAT WOULD REQUIRE DRINKING IT TOO.

AND WHERE HE'S FROM, IT WAS NORMAL FOR THEM TO LIVE ALONGSIDE HUMANS.

IT SEEMS THEY'LL ONLY DRINK A LITTLE BLOOD WHEN THEY NEED TO BOOST THEIR STRENGTH IN A DO-OR-DIE SITUATION.

I SEE... MAKES SENSE. IF HUMANS WENT EXTINCT, THEY'D LOSE THEIR MEALS.

HE ALSO SAID THAT TO CONVERT OTHERS, THEY NEED TO GIVE LARGE AMOUNTS OF THEIR OWN BLOOD OVER THE COURSE OF MANY YEARS, SO IT'S A BIG DECISION FOR THEM.

IF THEY DRINK TOO MUCH OF IT, IT'S ACTUALLY BAD FOR THEM.

MISAKI-CHAN WAS TURNED INTO A VAMPIRE IN A NON-TYPICAL WAY.

WHO'S TO SAY IF IT'S NECESSARILY NATURAL?

SO THERE'S A NATURAL MODERATION FUNCTION IN PLACE...YOU COULD SAY.

ANYWAY, GETTING BACK TO THE MAIN TOPIC...

KEE HEE HEE!

JUST LIKE A CYBORG!

IF HE USED MAGIC, HE COULD EASILY IMPROVE HER ARTIFICIALLY... OR RATHER, EVOLVE HER.

PAAAA (GLOOOOW)

LIKE A CYBORG!

SINCE THE PLACE HE COMES FROM HAS DRAGONS AND ALL KINDS OF OTHER CREA-TURES...

...IT MAKES SENSE THEY'D HAVE SOMETHING LIKE CYBORGS TOO, JUST TO ROUND IT OUT.

WH...

WHAT ARE YOU SAYING ...!?

I HAVE BOUND YOU TO A DRAGON'S FATE.

BUT IT WAS THE GREATEST PROOF OF MY TRUST THAT I COULD SHOW YOU.

I GOT YOU INVOLVED FOR MY OWN SAKE.

...I'M SORRY...

I TRUST YOU.

I SWEAR ON THE DRAGON WHOSE ARM THAT USED TO BE...

...AND ON YOUR MASTER, WHO ALLOWED ME TO DO THIS.

SO PLEASE FORM A PACT WITH ME...

LEND ME YOUR STRENGTH.

Whether you trust him or not, try having an honest heart-to-heart with him.

...IT'S HARD TO TRUST YOU, BUT AFTER SEEING THIS...

NOT TO MENTION THOSE TIGERS...

THAT SOUNDS LIKE SOMETHING A MONK ON A MOUNTAIN WOULD SAY...

I'VE BEEN TOLD THAT HALF OF A DRAGON'S FLESH IS SOMETHING OF AN AETHERIC BODY.

AS FOR HOW TO USE ITS FULL CAPABILITIES, I BELIEVE THE VESTIGES OF SOUL LEFT IN THE ARM WILL FILL YOU IN.

ONCE YOU GET USED TO IT, YOU SHOULD BE ABLE TO CONTROL ELECTRICITY WITH IT.

UNTIL THEN, IT MIGHT BE BEST NOT TO TOUCH PHONES AND SUCH WITH YOUR RIGHT HAND.

214

WHAT ...?

OH. THAT'S THE REAL POLKA-KUN.

AND THIS SHARK PLUSHIE IS...?

A MECHA ARM AND DRAGON ARM!

HM?

...And now the spoiled boy says he'd rather have a robot body than get his original body back.

Ha-ha... He means Polka is currently possessing that stuffed shark toy.

He seems to be enjoying himself in there... I was pretty dumbfounded myself.

I... SEE.

VERY WELL... YOUNG MASTER POLKA.

HYOI (YOINK)

?

UHH... HE SAYS HE LOOKS FORWARD TO GETTING ALONG WITH YOU, XIAOYU-KUN.

PEKO (BOW)

I LOOK FORWARD TO GETTING ALONG WITH YOU.

BEST REGARDS GOING FORWARD.

MECHA HAND! DRAGON HAND!

OOH!

YES!

ONE THING'S CERTAIN— WE'RE BEING TARGETED.

I-IN ANY CASE... I'M HAPPY FOR YOUR COOPERA-TION.

HUH? IS IT JUST ME OR IS HE EVEN MORE ANTAGONISTIC WITH POLKA THAN WITH ME?

...WHEN IT COMES TO THE ORGANIZATION AFFILIATED WITH THAT EMPIRE'S SIGIL...

...I WANT US TO PREPARE OURSELVES AS MUCH AS WE CAN.

LURING OUT THOSE WE REQUIRE IS YOUR FORTE...

...MOTH.

ALL WE CAN DO IS SET THINGS ON FIRE.

UMBRELLA: WATCH OUT FOR FIRES

...IS A BASTARD CHILD WHO CAME FROM THE OTHER SIDE OF THE SKY.

THEIR...

...ANCES-TOR...

A BUG EATING AWAY AT THIS WORLD.

THIS WILL BENEFIT YOU TOO.

...AS A MOTH WHO CRAVES THAT WHICH TRANSCENDS THE NATURAL LAWS.

OH?

...IS NOW ONE STEP...

...CLOS-ER.

WHAT YOU WANT...

ARE YOU SAYING...

...ALIENS...?

THE OTHER SIDE OF THE SKY...?

YOU SAY I'M ONE STEP CLOSER, BUT...DO YOU HAVE ANYTHING ELSE I CAN GO ON?

HMM...

NOR DO WE...

...CARE.

WE DON'T KNOW WHAT THE OTHER SIDE OF THE SKY IS EXACTLY.

...

...MOTH.

YOU SHOULD KNOW JUST AS WELL AS WE DO...

...IT'S ALL TIED TOGETHER SOMEWHERE... IS WHAT YOU'RE SAYING.

IF IT WAS NO COINCIDENCE AND MY AERIAL SHOW IS WHAT'S PUT EVERYTHING IN MOTION...

HEH HEH. THAT'S TRUE.

...OF COURSE, THAT INCLUDES YOU TOO.

FIRE-BREATH-ING BUG-KUN.

WHAT'RE YOU DOING?

GREAT. WE'LL BE GOING BACK AND FORTH BETWEEN HERE AND THE MAIN OFFICE FOR A WHILE, THOUGH.

I'M BACK.

REOR-GANIZING DATA.

THEY WERE NEVER FINISHED BEING DIGITIZED.

WE'RE REAPING THE REWARDS OF ALL THAT NEGLECT.

IT'S A DISCREDIT TO THE MATERIALS COMPILING GROUP.

YEAH, PRETTY OLD.

HMM...? OLD CASES?

THEN WHY AREN'T YOU USING A COMPUTER?

WHAT WE'RE FISHING FOR RIGHT NOW IS MORE ON FIRE-BREATHING BUG.

HUH? WASN'T THE CASE WITH SOLITAIRE JUST THREE YEARS AGO?

OR ARE YOU LOOKING INTO HIS PAST?

YOUR REACTIONS ARE AS MUTED AS EVER...

UH-HUH. AND WHY IS THAT?

BESIDES, THE TROUBLE-MAKERS ARE UNDER THE JURISDICTION OF US HERE AT COMPS-3.

BASTARD CHILD.

HABAKI HABAKI HABABABA KIKIKIKII!...

HE SAID IT. HE SAID IT.

HE SAIIIIID

IT'S NOT THAT.

ARE THEY ON DRUGS?

THESE GUYS!?

WITH AID FRIENDS?

WELL...

WE KNOW THAT HABAKI'S MEN AND FIRE-BREATHING BUG WERE IN OPPOSITION TO ONE ANOTHER.

WHICH MEANS WE NEED TO REVISIT EVERYTHING WE THINK WE KNOW ABOUT BUG...

PLUS SOLITAIRE AND FIRE-BREATHING BUG ARE CONNECTED.

-TON -TAP-

-TON

THE OFFICE OF A SMALL-TIME YAKUZA, ALONG WITH THE GANG LEADER AND FIVE MEMBERS, WENT UP IN FLAMES.

...HE WAS WITNESSED AT AN ARSON CRIME SCENE BELIEVED TO BE CAUSED BY FIRE-BREATHING BUG.

SHORTLY BEFORE SOLITAIRE LAUNCHED HIS DIRIGIBLE ...

I'M INNOCENT, SORRY!

222

IT NEVER GOT LEAKED TO THE MEDIA, BUT HE'S THE SECOND-MOST LIKELY SUSPECT.

THE FIRST BEING, OF COURSE, FIRE-BREATHING BUG.

APPARENTLY IT WAS A FIREFIGHTER WHO SAID HE SAW SOLITAIRE.

UNIT 1 AND THE YAKUZA WERE IN A FIT OVER IT.

...WELL, THAT'S WHEN THE MEDIA GAVE HIM HIS NAME, IN ANY CASE...

THE MYSTERY OF THE FIRE-BREATHING BUG

HIS TRUE I.D.

ONGOING INVEST

FIRE-BREATHING BUG HAS ONLY BEEN ON THE SCENE FOR THE PAST FEW YEARS.

...STILL, AREN'T THESE MATERIALS ANCIENT?

...IT SEEMS LIKE HE ONLY STARTED USING ENGLISH RECENTLY.

I ALSO FOUND THIS JUST THIS MORNING.

WALL: THIS WORLD IS FLAWED. AND SO IT SHOULD BE CONSUMED BY FLAME.

THAT MEANS FIRE-BREATHING BUG HAS BEEN AROUND SINCE WAY BEFORE I JOINED COMPS-3.

UMBRELLA: WATCH OUT FOR FIRES

KO (TAK)

KO

BUT...

...THEY...

...WILL NOT GO AWAY.

FOR 100 YEARS...

...WE...

...HAVE CONTINUALLY BURNED.

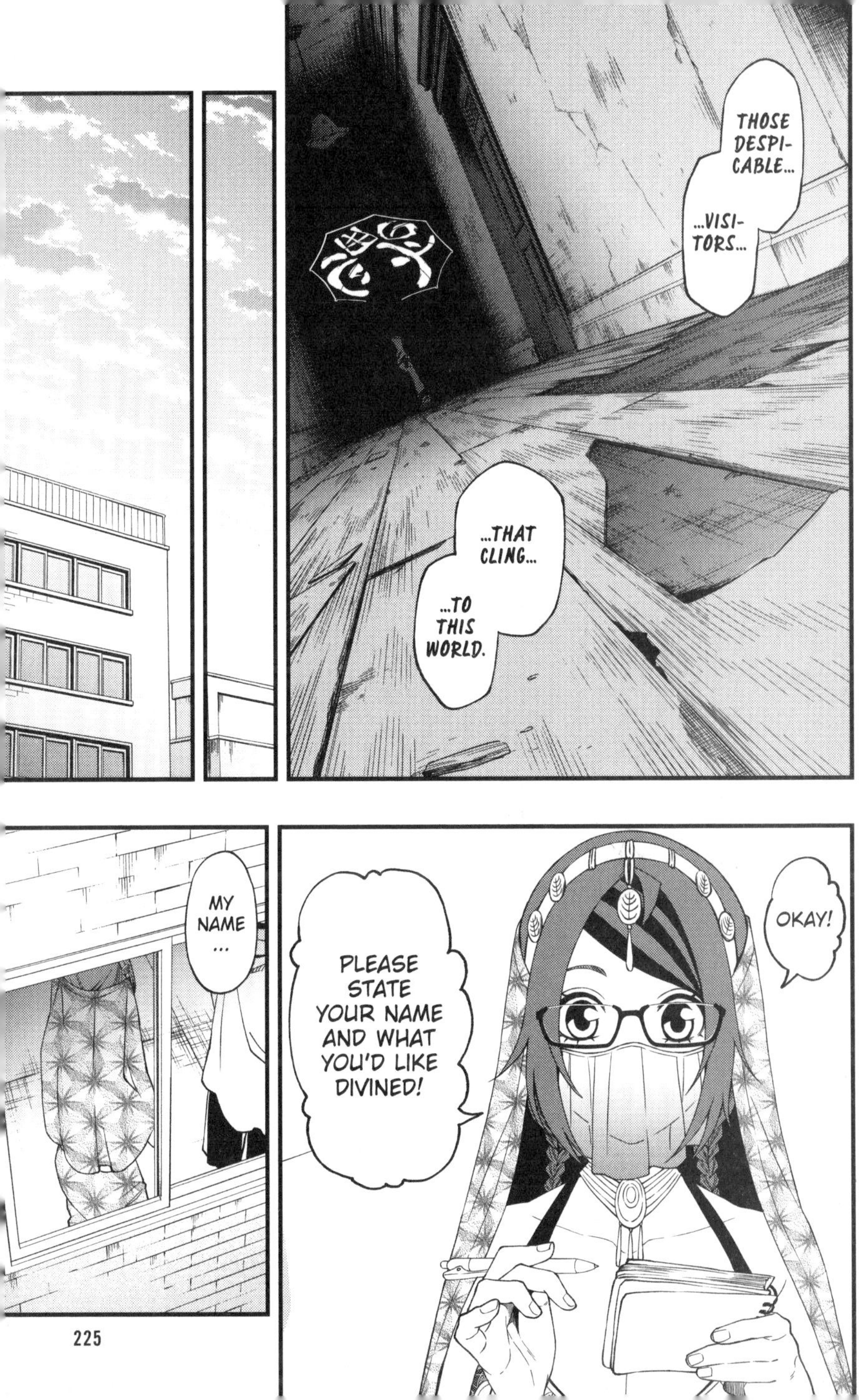
THOSE DESPI-CABLE...
...VISI-TORS...
...THAT CLING...
...TO THIS WORLD.
OKAY!
PLEASE STATE YOUR NAME AND WHAT YOU'D LIKE DIVINED!
MY NAME ...

PLEASE PUT DOWN "CIVIL."

AH, YES.

...I'D LIKE IT TO BE ABOUT "A FATE THAT THAT SPANS A HUNDRED YEARS" AND...

AS FOR WHAT I WANT DIVINED...

..."NEW ENCOUN-TERS."

DEAD MOUNT DEATH PLAY 7 END

TRANSLATION NOTES

COMMON HONORIFICS
no honorific: Indicates familiarity or closeness; if used without permission or reason, addressing someone in this manner would constitute an insult.
-san: The Japanese equivalent of Mr./Mrs./Miss. If a situation calls for politeness, this is the fail-safe honorific.
-sama: Conveys great respect; may also indicate the social status of the speaker is lower than that of the addressee.
-kun: Used most often when referring to boys, this indicates affection or familiarity. Occasionally used by older men among their peers, but it may also be used by anyone referring to a person of lower standing.
-chan: An affectionate honorific indicating familiarity used mostly in reference to girls; also used in reference to cute persons or animals of either gender.
-senpai: A suffix used to address upperclassmen or more experienced coworkers.
-sensei: A respectful term for teachers, artists, or high-level professionals.

[o]nee: Japanese equivalent to "older sis."
[o]nii: Japanese equivalent to "older bro."

CURRENCY CONVERSION
While exchange rates fluctuate daily, a good approximation is ¥100 to 1 USD.

Page 158
Yokai is the Japanese word for supernatural creatures. The minkirauwa is one such creature described in Japanese folklore that is said to steal a person's soul when it passes between their legs. Its name literally means "earless pig," and it is indeed depicted as a pig with no ears.

Page 209
The original pun for the Sharkspeare play used Shakespeare's Measure for Measure, with the Japanese for "measure" ("shaku") being elongated to sound like the English word "shark" ("shaaku").

DEAD MOUNT
DEATH PLAY

IT GOT RIPPED YESTERDAY, SO I'M GETTING A NEW ONE!

GOOD MORNING.

MISAKI-CHAN, YOU DON'T HAVE YOUR SWEATER TODAY.

NOT AS I AM NOW, BUT BEFORE I GOT THIS BODY, YEAH.

AREN'T YOU HOT, WEARING IT ALL THE TIME?

OOOH.

THESE TWO RARELY GO OUT.

AND MY SWEAT WOULD FREEZE.

BUT SOMETIMES ON THE TRAIN OR IN STORES, THE A/C MADE IT REALLY COLD.

228

IT WAS ALSO REALLY HANDY FOR CONCEALING WEAPONS AND CANDY IN.

DOESN'T THE WEIGHT OF IT CHOKE YOU?

I'M USED TO IT!

HOW DO YOU GET USED TO SOMETHING LIKE THAT?

SPECIAL THANKS!

WRITER:
RYOHGO NARITA

EDITOR:
KAZUHIDE SHIMIZU

TRANSLATION HELP:
JUYOUN LEE (YEN PRESS)

MAGIC RESEARCH:
KIYOMUNE MIWA
(TEAM BARREL ROLL)

STAFF:
YOSHICHIKA EGUCHI
YOSHIE YUNO
OTO
NANAMI HASAMA
NORA
YUMI

Turn to the back of the book to read an exclusive
bonus short story by Ryohgo Narita!

DEAD MOUNT DEATH PLAY

Episode ❼:
Order of a Parallel World

DEAD MOUNT DEATH PLAY 7

STORY: Ryohgo Narita   ART: Shinta Fujimoto

Translation: Christine Dashiell * Lettering: Abigail Blackman

DEAD MOUNT DEATH PLAY Volume 7 ©2021 Ryohgo Narita, Shinta Fujimoto/SQUARE ENIX CO., LTD. First published in Japan in 2021 by SQUARE ENIX CO., LTD. English translation rights arranged with SQUARE ENIX CO., LTD. and Yen Press, LLC through Tuttle-Mori Agency, Inc., Tokyo.

English translation ©2022 by SQUARE ENIX CO., LTD.

Yen Press
150 West 30th Street, 19th Floor
New York, NY 10001

Visit us at yenpress.com
facebook.com/yenpress
twitter.com/yenpress
yenpress.tumblr.com
instagram.com/yenpress

First Yen Press eBook Edition: April 2022
The chapters in this volume were originally published as ebooks by Yen Press.

Yen Press is an imprint of Yen Press, LLC.
The Yen Press name and logo are trademarks of Yen Press, LLC.

The publisher is not responsible for websites (or their content) that are not owned by the publisher.

Library of Congress Control Number: 2018953479

ISBNs: 978-1-9753-4064-3 (paperback)
       978-1-9753-4065-0 (ebook)

10 9 8 7 6 5 4 3 2 1

WOR

Printed in the United States of America

her address them, Shagrua realized that his hunch had been right all along.

"I thought you were past your assassination phase, remember? You failed in making the first attack. And I don't think it'd kill you to at least state your name," Izliz said, surveying the entire unit of countless red icicles floating in the air. "......Or would you rather I told Shagrua your name, Crimson Snow?"

In the next moment, the red icicles melted in the air and became a red snowstorm as they were drawn to a central point along the road. At the heart of that deep crimson snowstorm, a solitary shadow emerged.

"You're right. I did fail in my assassination...... I've realized this opponent will be difficult to launch a surprise attack on twice......"

The thin silhouette was illuminated by the light reflecting off the two satellites Zaji and Ruvu—or what the people of Earth would call "moonlight."

"There's no need to introduce myself, but......if I've already been found out, then......I suppose there's no point in hiding, either......"

The figure before Shagrua's eyes was a lone young woman dressed in a lavish white costume with a neat but carefully decorated hood covering the top half of her head.

"I took on the job to kill Shagrua-san...... My name is Silk Malacougar," she murmured, giving a polite salutation worthy of an aristocrat and casting a gloomy eye from below her hood.

Hearing her name, Shagrua immediately understood.

"Our time together will be short, but......I look forward to your kind consideration *for eternity*."

Standing before him was a powerful vampire counted among the enemies of the world.

Almost simultaneously, the room Shagrua had just been occupying was seeped in red. The imperial passageway was laid with bare cobblestones and patches of moss. Landing on the stones, Shagrua cast a silent spell to summon a light source to illuminate his surroundings, and he turned to the room now filled with red, his sword drawn and ready.

But when his heightened senses perceived the presence around him, Shagrua instantly changed tactics. With the help of an elementalist, he had made a contract with a Wind Elemental who had taken up residence in his spinal cord and whom he now awoke to spread out around him. An unseen vacuum blade enveloped Shagrua's body like a cyclone, repelling the countless red swarms that had flown toward him. Fragments of cobblestone leaped into the air and were instantly turned into a fine powder, a testament to the might of the gale blade.

However, the red came at Shagrua regardless, piercing right through the wind, and he cut it apart instantly.

There was a sound like a blend of metal and water as fragments of red struck the earth. Until just a moment before, the objects had been the shape of icicles, but they instantaneously became liquid, creating bloodred puddles on the flagstones.

Shagrua once again looked around. In the dark of night, Shagrua's magically conjured light illuminated...a multitude of red icicles poised in a full circle around him.

Is this a spell? But then where's the spell caster......? Wait, no. No, judging by this presence and the color of this soul, this is......!

Shagrua had noticed something, and he injected a powerful supply of mana into the Elementals that clad his body. Rather than perpetually intercepting them, Shagrua was building up a dense mana that seemed powerful enough to blow away anything in his vicinity. Faced with that, the swarm of red icicles froze.

The situation was at a deadlock for a few seconds—which was lifted at the hand of a third party.

"Good grief. If you're going to be violent, would you mind keeping it out of town?" came a voice from outside the swarm of red encircling Shagrua. It was a necromancer wearing a cow's skull over her head—Izliz Swordflail. "I don't mind the natural wear and tear, but I am rather attached to this place, so......I can't have you destroying it on me."

Izliz spoke to the red icicles, clearly a magical means of attack, and seeing

"The Saint of the Geldwood Church had drawn a plan for the fall of the empire a hundred years ago...... And that Saint is still alive......?"

Izliz was right. These were not things that could be believed so easily. If it had been anyone other than Shagrua, who had turned his back on the Geldwood Church and absconded, most followers would have rejected the idea without even waiting to hear them out.

And yet Shagrua, who had been used as the Church's final weapon, had never heard anything about any saint. The Church had nineteen head priests who held the top positions of power. It was true that about half of them were female, but none were called the Saint. If they had hidden that from even Shagrua, it strongly suggested that, for some reason, she was someone they could not allow to be publicly known.

Shagrua let out a sigh and muttered to himself as he sat down on his bed. "I guess I'll need to gather more intel...... If possible, I need to go to somebody who is in the know, someone who's not Izliz or any of her number. A third party independent from either the empire or the kingdom......"

As that last thought passed his lips, he fell quiet.

Without a sound, he expanded his awareness from his immediate surroundings to the entire room and then beyond its walls to the outside.

Despite being in the ruins of the fallen empire, he couldn't see any spectral beings even with his Evil Eye as Izliz evidently had taken some kind of measures against it. Perhaps it was due to his being in an environment that was so quiet for once that his senses were sharper than usual. That's why Shagrua had picked up on it. At first, it was simply a bad feeling in his gut. But by and by, he was certain something abnormal was going on.

Something's here.

It was different from Izliz or even Pirawizzo. Shagrua could feel a cold energy envelop his entire surroundings, and he focused harder to let his five senses melt into the room so as not to miss even the most subtle shift in the air currents.

It was deathly silent, as if time had stopped, and after several seconds had passed......Shagrua leaped into action. Grabbing the sword leaning by the window, he shattered the glass and instantly hurled his body through so that in less than the span of a single breath he was outside the dilapidated room.

inform you! They really are the lowest of the low! Whooee!"

"Hold on. Then, in other words......"

If Shagrua had left after becoming distrustful of the Church and had joined forces with those of the empire like Izliz, who had opposed the Church, then what might that mean?

"Shagrua-sama......could be a sole aggressor or protector in the eyes of those from the empire......"

"It's ironic, isn't it? While the Corpse God-kun crossed over to the world without the use of the hole—"

Pani paused and narrowed her eyes, gazing at the image of Earth being projected in the air. "The man who killed him, Shagrua-kun, is about to be caught up in the struggle over that hole!"

■■■

The Abandoned Peninsula, ruins of the Imperial Capital, night.

"An alternate world, huh......? It's hard to suddenly believe in something like that."

Shagrua had temporarily taken shelter in one of the ruins that had been repaired just enough to be livable and was reviewing all the information he'd been given over the past few days, trying to wrestle it into order.

Of it all, what he had been told regarding an "alternate world" that Izliz Swordflail and the "Poisonous Dragon of Destruction" Pirawizzo loomed foremost in his mind.

"I've never seen for myself what kind of place the alternate world would be like. From what those in the know have said, it sounds like they have their fair share of interesting things: iron vessels that fly through the sky faster than the speed of sound and devices that allow you to speak to people on the other side of the world. Romelka was pretty interested in something called movies herself."

"Kuh-kuh. But for a magic user like you, a world so faint in aether would probably make you feel frustrated, Wandering Balcony. Then again, as a necromancer, as long as the land has death, you'd probably make do."

"In any case, the goons at the Geldwood Church are attempting to once again force open the hole here, where the space is so unstable. I don't expect you to simply believe us, but now that you're involved, you'd better think about how you're going to conduct yourself from here on out."

intentions were when he migrated or even if it was something he did on purpose or just by chance."

"I......see."

As far as Recuria was concerned, the Corpse God was an enemy of the world. But having seen the actions Shagrua had taken, she couldn't deny the fact that doubts had started to manifest in her heart.

In battle, Corpse God took the form of a giant freakish skeleton, and the way he said and did things didn't make him seem like a very benevolent being. Even assuming he had some kind of ulterior plan, there was no way to ascertain what it was. The texts that Shagrua had been able to read appeared to have been written in a unique alphabet decipherable only by those with the Evil Eye. But these had been sealed away by the upper echelons of the Geldwood Church, not to mention that as she was basically a runaway at this point, she couldn't look into it.

"And just what does Sir Shagrua have to do with all this?"

"Aah! I'll tell you that now, too! Granted, I don't know if you'll believe me as a clergy member of the Geldwood Church, but the last time the man-made path to Earth was opened, the spell was performed using the combined forces of the Geldwood Church and a faction of the empire! And that was over a hundred years ago!"

"Huh......?"

"Anyway, it's not quite accurate to call it a path since it's really just a hole! And if one were *entertaining the idea of getting rid of the empire while they were at it*, that probably would be the best way to do the deed!"

What Pani said was shocking, and Recuria's brain did its best to struggle to make sense of the information she'd just been told.

But she still didn't see what that had to do with Shagrua. As though to give her a further hint, Pani smiled daringly and continued.

"The ruins of the empire are now being guarded by Izliz-san and her kind, to keep the hole from being opened again. ......Now, Izliz-san and company aren't enough to pose a real threat to the Church...... But if the world's most powerful military force were to take even one step in the direction of that Abandoned Peninsula, what do you think would happen?"

"......! You're not saying that Shagrua-sama......is in the Abandoned Peninsula?!"

"I detected him there, and the Geldwood Church has monitored Shagrua's magic powers for many years, so those in the highest positions of power are sure to have figured that out by now. Though I take it they didn't care to could pass through it over years and years—possibly to blend each other's plant life, atmospheres, microbiomes, and environments!"

"U-um, wait a second. I'm not following......"

"Sure, I'll wait! I'll wait however many years or even decades it takes for you to understand this! 'Cos we're friends!"

"......When you were first explaining it to me, you flew into a rage and told me, 'If you can't even comprehend this, then you are one fascinating specimen!' remember?" Utsurojuza interjected with a scowl on his face.

Pani answered unexpectedly with, "I wasn't enraged. I was serious! And it was thanks to you becoming my friend, Shula-kun, that I realized how far superior my brain is to others! Thanks! Now that I understand the difference between myself and others, I know what I'm about! I'll wait however long it takes for Recu-chan to catch up! Heh-heh!"

"I'm sorry about her. This is just who she is, you see? But I'm real sorry, okay?"

Utsurojuza's apology seemed sincere, but Recuria wasn't sure how best to respond. However, before she could say anything, Pani continued on.

"The question is, *which originated first*: life and humanity in this world or on Earth? Was it that humans were first born on Earth and then migrated over here? Or were they born here and migrated to Earth......? Well, let's just leave that question to the archeologists, historians, and magisters! I'm just developing new technologies for the sake of a pleasant future! I've got magic in my left hand! And engineering in my right! I am 'The Alchemy Scholar' Pani!"

For whatever reason, Pani had launched into a self-introduction mixed with propaganda.

She then got her breathing back under control and said to Recuria with a serious look on her face, "Now then, before you understand the relationship and history between Earth and our world, let me just say this: Corpse God's soul was transported over to the planet called Earth. I was able to figure that out because I had already speculated as to whether it would be possible for a path to materialize unexpectedly. This is just a conjecture, but...... that place you call 'the great beyond' might be connected to Earth's 'great beyond'! Therefore, in the soul state, he may have succeeded in migrating over without any intervention from Ordom!"

"His soul......went to another world? Are you saying that Corpse God revived there?!"

"Unfortunately, I can't say for sure! I don't know what Corpse God's

more three-dimensional than that and looked just like a semi-transparent, colorful pattern was floating in space.

"I-is this......an illusion?"

"It's the power of this instrument! Though if you were to combine the spell of far-sight with an illusion, you'd be able to do pretty much the same thing!" Pani replied, continuing to trace her finger along the desk's glass sheet. Doing so caused the three-dimensional aerial projected image to undergo a change, and a glowing red sphere took form alongside various other smaller colored spheres that began to orbit around it at different speeds.

"When I compared the 'beyond' with our world, the relationship between its fixed star and planets is no different from ours! From what I've observed, the same goes for its relationship within an even greater star cluster!"

"What is this......?"

"Not so fast—there's no need to rush!" Pani said, smiling cheerfully, and she used the transparent board to initiate an operation so that the projection changed yet again.

The spheres orbiting what evidently was a fixed star were enlarged, and the other images disappeared as though pushed out of the frame. The image closed in on a sphere of blue, green, and brown mixed with white.

A white sphere was orbiting around it as it rotated, and for a moment, Recuria thought it might be an image of their own planet until—

"Only one satellite.....? And......the shapes of the landmasses are completely different......"

"Yep! This isn't Zaji or Ruvu! Earth's satellite is called the moon! And this sphere with colors so similar to our own planet......is the very same Earth that we've been talking about!" Pani said as she proudly puffed out her chest. "Within the sea of stars on the other side—which is very different from our own—the number of heavenly bodies that could support life is, from what I've discovered, 275! Of course, one could speculate that it's actually more like over several tens of billions, but I don't have time to be searching them all! And of all those heavenly bodies, there's one that's special! The only planet connected by a path to our world is this here Earth! It's simply sublime! Exquisite! Tasty-looking!"

"You wanna eat it? Are you serious?"

Ignoring Utsurojuza's reproachful remark, Pani narrowed her eyes and addressed Recuria. "......Of course, it's not as though I was the one who linked the path. An ancient culture from way, way, way before I was born is the one that connected it! And it's such a wide path that an entire country

From behind the puzzled Recuria came the voice of "Utsurojuza" Shula Zoozolozo Cramplamp Lampton sounding annoyed: "Uhh...... You can ignore her, okay? For someone who's lived so long, she's got relatively few friends, you know? She's just got herself all excited over making a new friend, see?"

"Aah! Right you are! Wow, Shula-kun! Spoken like one of my true few, scant friends! In any case, I've put the cart before the horse, but that's okay since Recuria-kun is my friend now! Seeing as how you've heard about Earth now, I'm making you my friend whether you like it or not! I'm really stubborn, so just give it up!"

"Are you pressuring her into being your friend? I don't care so much about me, but don't you think you're putting Recuria in a difficult position?"

Without even protesting having been called one of her "few, scant friends," Shula muttered this while casting his tired eyes at the instruments and such in the corners of the room.

Worried that she would never make progress otherwise, Recuria attempted to direct the flow of the conversation. "U-um! If you'll have me, I'd love to be your friend, so please do tell me more! About the Corpse God and......what he has to do with Shagrua-sama."

"Friendship established! Man, you've struck a good deal! Since I imagine Shula-kun will point this out anyway, I'll just clarify ahead of time that the definition of 'friendship,' in my opinion, depends on whether both parties agree to it! I don't care if it's a friendship that can be bought with money! I'll put a high price on it! Friendship is worth its weight in gold! But true friendship is the kind that doesn't come with a price! The possibility for friendship is always endless! A big win!"

As Pani grasped her hand and shook it up and down, Recuria wondered how the individual before her could really be called one of the "enemies of the world." However, now was not the time to get caught up on such questions, and she decided to hold her tongue and listen to what the girl had to say.

"Now, then! You wanted to know about Corpse God-kun, right, Recu-chan? Though it might actually be 'Calamity Crusher' Shagrua Edith Lugrid-kun whom you're more concerned with!"

With that, she turned on her heel and headed for a strange white desk in the back of the room. There, she traced a finger along what looked like a glass surface set within it, causing it to glow. At the same time, the inside of the room grew darker, and in the space between the ceiling and floor—precisely in the center of the room—a form made of light appeared. It very much resembled a magic circle hanging in the air during spell casting, but it was

They say that up until a thousand years ago, it was frequently connected with this world.

They say that in order to open the pathway between the two worlds, special magic and technology is required, but those have since been lost.

They say that because of this, only the "Destructive Wyvern" Ordom is capable of opening that path at present.

They say that Ordom doesn't have much interest in that alternate world, so he only very rarely does.

They say that the last time Ordom opened the path, the sixth member of the Federation of Latham, The Artisan, was transferred over.

They say that land used to be called Terra Mater.

They say that that land is now called Earth.

Inside Pani's Aerial Studio.

"Yeah, Earth! 地球! Земля! γη! Terra, Terre, Tierra, Terra!"

The "Alchemy Scholar" Pani Guldmarg went careening around the room, spouting a litany of strange languages that sounded like an incantation; somewhat taken aback, Recuria Lofilardo only managed to murmur the first:

"Urth......"

"Oh, right! Out of respect for Shula-kun, let's all agree to call it Earth! Granted, compared to the world we live in, it sure seems to have a lot of languages! In our case, we might have been influenced to unify our languages into one for the sake of invoking spells. In recent years, Earth has been developing 'programming languages' or some such that seem to be spreading across cultures. But I see, I see! They may not have magic, but they do have a language that controls mechanical devices! Amazing! Just marvelous!"

Recuria was at a loss, not sure what there was to be so happy about, while Pani continued to squirm with glee, flapping her hands overhead. She stepped up to Recuria.

"Come on—you do it too!"

"Huh? Oh. Okay."

Doing as she was told, Recuria raised both hands up, and Pani smacked her own palms against them with a sharp little slap.

"Excellent! A wonderful sound! Absolutely fantastic! Done like a true friend!"

"R-right."

DEAD MOUNT DEATH PLAY

Episode ❼: Order of a Parallel World

by Ryohgo Narita

Manga exclusive bonus short story

This world is not alone.

In the world Shagrua and his people inhabit, those words have been a familiar refrain since the days of old. This other world is thought to have vastly different technologies and beliefs that are continually tested, and even now its waters house ancient sea monsters that were once revered as divine beasts.

Some speak of it with adoration, imagining it to be something akin to an ideal paradise, while some fear it as a land of exiled criminals and still others simply laugh it off as a fairy tale.

However, even though the tale was the stuff of legend, it was not so widely known as most fairy tales. The story of the other world was told within the circles of religions that have persisted since olden times, the ruling families who have held power for centuries, and the dragons who have lived since ancient times; it was an exceptionally rare "fairy tale" known only to a chosen few.

They say that the world exists on the reverse side of the celestial sphere.

They say that the aether there is weak and the land has few Elementals.

They say that it has a spherical island floating in its sky, which is called by various names.

They say that sphere might be a satellite similar to this world's very own Zaji and Ruvu.

They say that while the world itself remains the same, it has gone through a number of different phases.

They say that at the very least, human culture has had a presence there for thousands of years.